The North of
FRANCE

ST OMER: The canal-side road to Dunkerque

The North of FRANCE

A Guide to the Art, Architecture, Landscape and
Atmosphere of Artois, Picardy and Flanders

Michael Barker & Paul Atterbury

A Road in Picardy by Sir Frank Brangwyn

The Heyford Press

For Audrey Atterbury and Maureen Barker

The authors are grateful to Jeremy Lewis for putting the text on the right course, to Sue Whitaker, Karen Bailey and Melanie Davis for typing the manuscripts and to Jennifer Kavanagh who battled to encourage publishers to appreciate The North of France.

All photographs were taken by the authors except for the following, reproduced by kind permission of the French Government Tourist Office, Piccadilly:
Amiens (The cathedral and the gilded Virgin p. 24) Villers-Bretonneux (Australian memorial p. 28) Thiepval (Memorial to the Missing p. 35) Arras (Beaux-Arts Museum p. 42) Béthune (Grand'Place p. 61) Etaples (War memorial p. 133) St Amand-les-Eaux (The abbey tower p. 135)

Vauban (p. 138) by courtesy of Hopkins Antiques Ltd., Cuckfield, Sussex.

Cover: *Etaples, 1914* by G.L. Hunter (Private Collection)
reproduced by kind permission of The Fine Arts Society, Glasgow.
Title Page: *A Road in Picardy 1903* by Sir Frank Brangwyn
reproduced by kind permission of Austin/Desmond Fine Art, London.
Abbeville 1819 and *Boulogne 1819* by Capt. Robert Batty
reproduced on pages 6 amd 142 by kind permission of Wildenstein & Co, London.

A CIP catalogue record for this book is available from the British Library.

ISBN 1 873330 00 6
First published in 1990
by the Heyford Press, London

© Michael Barker and Paul Atterbury

Printed in Great Britain by Flaydemouse, Yeovil, Somerset.

Distributed by Richard Dennis Publishing, The Old Chapel, Shepton Beauchamp, nr Ilminster, Somerset TA19 0LE.
Tel. 0460 42009

CONTENTS

PREFACE

This is not a conventional guide of the kind that directs its readers to hotels, restaurants, shops, amusements for children, or other tourist facilities. All this information is readily available, and the traveller should set out equipped with the good basic essentials listed at the end of the book. *The North of France* is a straightforward alphabetically arranged gazeteer of the main towns, plus excursions to nearby places of interest.

It is specifically aimed at the visually alert and curious traveller who seeks the unusual and requires information which is not otherwise easily obtainable. It is a book about atmosphere and incident, and often strays off the beaten track, but without ignoring the principal attractions. The selection is personal, and the entries often concentrate on the eccentric or unusual. We include all those places or items that we think deserve attention, including some which have either fallen out of fashion or are not yet in fashion and are certainly not mentioned in conventional guides. These include public sculpture and memorials; Art Nouveau and Art Deco buildings; shop fronts; tile panels and decorative lettering, pre- and post-war churches, and modern stained glass. Many of the visual minutiae of daily life are being all too readily swept away in England. France is generally a more conservative country, but increasing affluence is noticeably affecting the endearing, old-fashioned character which is one of its great attractions. Mass tourism has not yet reached the North of France, but the Channel Tunnel will almost certainly bring changes, and the crowds. This guide will point you in the right direction if you want to seek out the unusual, and the vulnerable, before the region is swamped.

When planning tours bear in mind that museums are usually closed on Tuesdays and the opening hours are fairly restrictive – usually 10 am until noon and 2 pm until 5 pm. A number of museums are being re-planned and modernised, so that some closures are inevitable. But to compensate there are impressive plans for new museums at Dunkerque, Boulogne, Péronne, Calais and Abbeville. It is advisable before leaving to check with the French National Tourist Office for up-to-date information.

The long lunch break is still the general rule in France, with the result that shops and tourist offices are almost certain to be shut from noon or 12.30 for two hours. Churches are now often closed except for services, but the keys are usually close at hand – it is best to ask in the nearest shop or café. Many shops are closed on Monday mornings, but food shops are open on Sunday mornings, and until later in the day than is usual in England. The rhythm of life is different, and it is necessary to adapt to avoid frustration. The ubiquitous café will provide snacks such as sandwiches and *croques-monsieur* at all hours, and of course the licensing laws present no problems so that a glass of wine or a carafe (usually *un quart*) is always available. In the provinces particularly, restaurants start to serve lunch at noon, and it is wise to arrive before 1 pm to ensure a meal. The serving of dinner generally starts at 7.30 pm and the chef usually stops at 9 pm, except in *brasseries* which nearly always announce their serving times on the menu – placed, as the law decrees, outside the restaurant. Be warned that Sunday lunch is a popular time for families to eat together, so one should book in advance, also that many restaurants are closed on Sunday or Monday evenings. In high season it is unwise to arrive in search of a hotel room much after 6.30 pm. To be on the safe side, make good use of the tourist guides recommended in the bibliography, and anticipate your needs.

An enjoyable way to appreciate local life is to participate in the many towns and village events – look out for posters which announce *foires, braderies, ducasses, défiles* or *fêtes*.

Abbeville 1819 by Capt Robert Batty

INTRODUCTION

A few years ago, returning from a working assignment in the Loire Valley, we decided to make a detour on the way to Calais to visit the region of the Somme. In the evening we came to Roye, a small town barely mentioned in any guide book, and discovered an outstanding yet unknown Art Deco church. The meandering route we took the next day revealed more Art Deco churches and hôtels de ville (town halls), some delightful old shop fronts and cafés, 1950s stained glass and sculpture, several châteaux, medieval to nineteenth century, other interesting examples of Renaissance, Baroque and eighteenth-century architecture, and the simply astonishing power and quality of the great war memorials of the Somme. All this confirmed that the North of France was full of the most extraordinary visual rewards.

Visits to local bookshops and tourist offices made it abundantly clear that much of this material was not concisely documented, and thus largely unknown to visitors with both specialist and more general tastes. The few books that claimed to cover the region dealt only in the obvious and were, more often than not, written by people who had never used their eyes, and who sometimes referred even to things which had long disappeared.

Yet there is probably no part of France that sees as many visitors as the North. Over 15 million people pass through each year, but very few bother to stop and explore. For most people the North of France is simply a stretch of motorway or trunk road to be traversed as quickly as possible on the way to somewhere else. The result is that millions of people miss the chance to enjoy a part of France that is unique in its variety and quality of architecture and landscape, and in the importance of its history.

The chance discovery of the church at Roye prompted us to explore the North of France as thoroughly as possible, and to produce the visual guide that the region clearly needed. This caused some raising of eyebrows among various friends and colleagues, several of whom expressed the standard British point of view that we were wasting our time as there was little of interest in the North of France. Our aim in this book is to overturn such prejudices and to convince its readers to do likewise, to put aside everything they have ever been told and plunge into the unknown. We can guarantee that it will be worthwhile, for there is far more to the North of France than Amiens Cathedral. A certain prejudice exists also in the mind of the average Frenchman who considers le Nord flat, windswept and dreary in winter, a region which produces no wine and, apart from sending its fish to the parts of France which count, has little of interest. As with all prejudices there is some truth and much unfairness. In gastronomic matters the region is just as obsessed with food as elsewhere in France. You will find excellent mussels, usually cooked in white wine, dishes using with imagination the locally produced beer and gin, winter vegetables such as endives and cauliflowers (a speciality of St Omer), *andouillette* sausages, game pâtés, river eels *en croute* and so on.

The North of France, le Nord to the French, does *not* mean a geographical area of France above a certain latitude which would include Brittany and Normandy. It specifically means the old provinces of Artois, Picardy and Flanders. These are now covered by the *départements* – administrative areas created after the Revolution – of Nord, Pas-de-Calais and Somme and the northern parts of the Oise and the Aisne. The area covered by this book is more tightly drawn: roughly a hundred-mile radius from Calais. Thus it excludes the southern part of Picardy which includes the towns of Beauvais, Compiègne and Soissons, all historically in the province, but since the Revolution considered a part of the Ile-de-France – the region surrounding Paris, somewhat akin to the Home Counties of London. Laon is also excluded, nowadays more aligned to the Champagne region. It is noticeable however that for touristic reasons, the old provinces have been revived.

Regional characteristics may not be immediately apparent to a newcomer to France, who may imagine it to be one country with a single language; but this is certainly not the case. Although France projects a strong external image of its 'Frenchness', and of its culture and language – a major invisible export as it were – it is actually an amalgamation, over the centuries, of many territories with different ethnic backgrounds and languages. The national boundaries have changed many times – indeed as recently as the 1930s. A French man is more likely to regard himself as a Picard, or a Flamand, first and foremost.

The three ancient provinces which form the subject of this book have quite separate characteristics, fashioned by history and with different ethnic backgrounds. The northern frontier of France was created by Louis XIV and artificially bisects Flanders whose people are of the Low Countries; they are Germanic in origin, and their first language is Flemish, not French. Their art and architecture belonged to the tradition of the Low Countries and continued to do so until modern times – as evidenced, for example, by the Flemish character of their towns rebuilt after the Great War. But southern Flanders, the Cambrésis, whose capital is Cambrai, is Walloon, and French predominates. There is a parallel in neighbouring Belgium – a modern state – which is strongly divided between Flemish-speakers in the north and French-speakers, Walloons, in the south.

The inland province of Artois has a less clear ethnic identity, but is nevertheless almost as Flemish as French. Arras, the capital is decidedly Flemish, notably in its architecture. Both Artois and Flanders were ruled by the Dukes of Burgundy until the end of the fifteenth century, followed by alliances or marriages which gave power over these provinces to the Austro-Spanish House until the Treaty of the Pyrenees of 1659. One legacy of this period was the building of Renaissance bailliages, seats of local government under Spanish rule.

Picardy, although a welding together of many fiefs, was finally united with the kingdom of France after 1477. It has always had a strong regional sense; its own language, related to Old French, is still spoken as a *patois*, and is now undergoing a modest revival as a specific language.

Geographically, the North of France is defined by the natural border of the North Sea and the frontier with Belgium to the north, by the Champagne to the east, the Ile-de-France to the south and Normandy and the English Channel to the west.

It is a commonly expressed prejudice that the North of France is flat, industrial and boring, but wider exploration will show that this general condemnation is totally unjustified. The region is mostly undulating and rural, with industry situated in well defined areas which are not without their own interest. It is hard to travel more than a few miles in any direction without coming upon something stimulating. The architectural choice is wide ranging, and probably more diverse than in any other area of comparable size in the whole of France. One finds great Gothic churches and abbeys, medieval châteaux, fortified towns, the military architecture of the great Vauban, many eighteenth-century châteaux, excellent fine and decorative art museums, Baroque town architecture, industrial archaeology, Art Nouveau, Art Deco, Moderne and contemporary buildings, and a variety of vernacular architecture in diverse building materials.

In the aftermath of the Great War the people of the North rebuilt their shattered towns, villages and farms with great courage and spirit. Towns such as Bailleul display a revival of traditional Flemish architecture, re-interpreted for the twentieth century, while the particular English genius of the era contributed an astonishing concentration of monuments, sculpture and landscape architecture, notably at Thiepval and Villers-Bretonneux. And the Canadian memorial at Vimy is a powerful and original design, and a major work of twentieth-century Expressionist monumental sculpture.

The two principal industrial areas are the Lille-Roubaix-Tourcoing conglomeration (textiles, steel, chemicals and brewing) close to the Belgium border, and the mining belt between Béthune and Valenciennes (coal, steel and car manufacture). There are also pockets of industry centered on the larger towns of Dunkerque (petro-chemicals and steel), Amiens, Arras and St Quentin; they were historically based on textiles, though a changing world has brought newer industries such as electronics.

Traditional industries are still in situ: ceramics at Desvres, glass-making at Arques, velvet at Amiens and cast iron for stoves and cooking-ware at Guise. The canals and navigable rivers remain an important means of transportation of the industrial and agricultural production.

The landscape varies enormously and can change abruptly. Most of it is over 100 metres above sea level. The flat lands are found in Northern Flanders close to the sea, the fertile marshy plain, with its network of dykes, is dotted with windmills and is also relatively treeless, so that the tall church towers and proud belfries, symbols of hard-won civic liberties, are prominent under the big skies. But hills are not lacking: they spring up suddenly, at Cassel and Mont des Cats for example.

The distinct flavour of the Low Countries is ever present. Villages have names such as Bollezeele, Zutkerque and Godewaersvelde. Beer-drinking and a heavy *cuisine* are the staple of the region, whose inhabitants are often Flemish-speakers. Stepped gables, decorative brickwork and tall spiky buildings of dark brick form the backcloth. Many of them, however, are products of the 1920s rebuilding programme after war damage. This neo-Flemish style, although conservative and even anachronistic, was part of a fervent and romantic revivalism, a nostalgia for a Flanders as it was before the Spanish occupation – which, in architectural terms left its own mark most elegantly, notably in the Renaissance bailliages of Aire-sur-la-Lys and Hesdin, the Baroque Old Bourse at Lille, and the arcaded Grand'Place at Arras.

The countryside inland from Boulogne, known as the Boulonnais, is hilly and scattered with woodland where wild boar and deer still roam. Farming is on a small scale. Villages of white cottages with orange pantiled roofs nestle in the numerous pretty river valleys. The towns, such as Montreuil and Hesdin, are quite small, each with a mere 3,000 inhabitants, of intimate scale, and quite distant from each other.

Artois is generally more open: undulating plains, watered by rivers such as the Scarpe, are overlooked by wooded ridges like Vimy. From Béthune to Valenciennes agriculture intersperses with mining. But in pockets the industry is dense, under skies of gun-metal grey it can sometimes be a melancholy area to visit, suffused with an atmosphere evoked in Emile Zola's novel *Germinal*.

Eastwards from Cambrai the landscape is dominated by vast rolling plains, cultivated with sugar beet and corn. Patches of woodland, and then forest, become more frequent towards the dense wooded hills of the Ardennes over the border in Belgium. The high plateaux of Picardy are broad treeless prairies with vast horizons, cut through by the verdant, sometimes marshy, river valleys of the Somme, the Authie and the Canche, rich territory for the angler. Towards Normandy the landscape becomes dense with small lush pastures, apple orchards for cider-making, and thick woods of oak and beech.

The coastline of the North extends for some two hundred kilometres. From Dunkerque to Calais it is flat, scrubby and frankly dreary. However, south of Calais, from the Channel Tunnel works to Boulogne, the undulating D940 road climbs the high cliffs and swoops down into the valleys to provide an exhilarating journey.

From Boulogne the D940 runs southwards and inland from an unexciting coast of sand dunes and modest family resorts of little visual interest – save, perhaps for the relatively larger town of Le Touquet.

The Bay of the Somme, however, is splendid. The charming resorts and fishing ports of Le

Crotoy and St Valery-sur-Somme face each other across the vast expanse of the bay, which is an important natural reserve for migratory birds. Three-quarters of all known European species have been sighted here. These descriptions are of a very general nature and conceal many anomalies and sudden contrasts. It is not uncommon to cross over hills straddled by grim terraces of miners' housing and then drop into a lush valley, where a pretty village is clustered around a medieval fortress. After passing through a beech forest, a broad plain appears, dominated by a concrete grain silo of cathedral proportions, while on the horizon the eccentric outline of a water tower and its bright abstract paintwork is visible. In the middle ground the towers of a Gothic church and a belfry rise above the old roof-tops of a town; on its edge post-war residential tower blocks form a hard, banal frame.

The North of France has often lain in the path of invaders, some looking across the Channel to England. Julius Caesar and his legions sailed from Boulogne to conquer England. A thousand years later William the Conqueror followed suit, raising anchor at St Valery-sur-Somme. In 1803 Napoleon established an enormous army camp at Boulogne for his planned invasion of England. He reportedly declared that 'if we are masters of the Channel for six hours, we will rule the world' but a fortuitous advance by the Austrians diverted his army to Bavaria.

The claims of Edward III of England to the French crown led to his invasion of France in 1339 and the beginning of the Hundred Years War. A decisive victory at Crécy (1346) and the occupation of Calais (the famous Rodin sculpture of the Burghers of Calais records this humiliation) mark the early English domination in the war. Edward subsequently renounced his claims to the French throne but gained Aquitaine. The other decisive English victory of the Hundred Years War also took place in the region – that of Henry V at the bloody battle of Agincourt in 1415 when, in a single day, a whole generation of French nobility was wiped out, after which the English occupied a large part of France.

In 1431 Henry VI of England was crowned King of France and the betrayed heroine, Joan of Arc, was burned at the stake in Rouen by the English. But by the end of the century England had lost all its possessions in France except Calais, and France began to move from a medieval social system towards a more modern state.

The new ideas of the Renaissance filtered into France from Italy during the reign of François I (1515–47), a time when much building took place at Blois, Chambord, the Louvre and Fontainebleau. It was a period of increasing menace from Spain who now possessed the Netherlands, Flanders and Artois. In 1520, to counter this threat, François met Henry VIII of England at the Field of the Cloth of Gold, near Calais, but an *entente* was not concluded.

The French finally expelled the English from French soil, with the capture of Calais by the Duc de Guise in 1558. The second half of the century saw the spread of the ideas of Martin Luther and Jean Calvin (not a Swiss as often assumed, but a Picard from Noyon), and the growing strength of Protestantism in France led to the civil wars of religion. Two thousand Huguenots were killed in the Massacre of the Eve of St Bartholomew in 1572.

Henry IV (1589–1610), a Bourbon, came to the throne a Protestant, but for political reasons accepted the Catholic faith. The Edict of Nantes (1598) established toleration of Protestant worship. Henry's daughter, Henrietta Maria, married Charles I of England. The gallant Henry, known to have had fifty-six mistresses, was assassinated in Paris and his son Louis XIII (1610–1643) came to the throne, supported and much influenced by Cardinal Richelieu. The Cardinal ruthlessly renewed the persecution of the Protestant Huguenots and can be said to have changed the monarchy of France from being feudal to absolute. This absolutism was epitomised by the rule of Louis XIV the Sun King, from 1643 to 1715. He waged more than thirty costly campaigns, largely with the aim of tidying up the boundaries of France, particularly in the North. Artois was ceded by Spain in 1659, and the short sharp campaign of 1667–8 secured several towns in Flanders. Victory assured, he commissioned the military architect Vauban to fortify the frontier towns of Dunkerque, Bergues, Lille, Valenciennes, le Quesnoy and Maubeuge. A second line of defence was established by the fortification of Gravelines, St Omer, Aire, Béthune, Arras, Douai and Cambrai. The legacy of Vauban's ingenious and dramatic star-shaped bastions may still be seen today, notably at Lille and Arras.

The northern boundaries of modern France were fixed by the Treaty of Utrecht in 1713. The end of the extravagant reign of Louis XIV, which had seen the building of the great Palace of Versailles and which was also a golden age of French literature and culture was, however, less glorious. Louis XIV's ambition was to conquer the Low Countries, but in the battles of the War of the Spanish Succession (1701–14) his troops suffered defeats at the hands of Marlborough and Prince Eugéne at Blenheim (1704), Ramillies (1706), Oudenaarde (1708) and Malplaquet (1709).

The Sun King's great-grandson, the idle Louis XV ('après moi, le deluge'), ruled from 1715–1774, but as a minor, under a Regency until 1723. This was an era when fighting for *la gloire* became increasingly ruinous. The prosperous colonies in India, North America and the West Indies were lost. The extravagance and negligence of the Court, the impending financial ruin, and the spread of ideas of *liberté*, partly emanating from America, and the influence of anti-establishment philosophers, all sowed the seeds of revolution.

Louis XVI acceded in 1774 with his unpopular wife, Marie Antoinette, an Austrian. He was too weak a ruler to carry out reforms which might have solved the financial crises and eased the general unrest, exacerbated by bad harvests and the costly support for the American struggle for independence from Britain.

The result was the French Revolution – instigated by the middle-class rather than the proletariat. The Bastille was stormed in 1789 and the Reign of Terror ensued, with the ferocious guillotine claiming thousands of lives, most notably those of Louis and his wife. Robespierre, born in Arras and his infamous friend Lebon, mayor of the city, beheaded many people of Artois, but the eventual reaction to the bloodshed led to both their executions.

The last years of the century saw the rise of Napoleon, and his military success in Europe which isolated England. The Peace of Amiens concluded between England and France in 1802 was merely a lull in hostilities. Napoleon had already prepared an invasion of England from Boulogne. Created Emperor in 1804, his powerful reign finally came to an end with defeat at the Battle of Waterloo of 1815.

The Bourbons were then restored as rulers, Louis XVIII (1814–24) arriving at Calais to great acclamation. His period of limited monarchy was called the Restoration. He was succeeded by Charles X (1824–1830) but the Revolution of 1830 – ignited by rebellion against his reactionary policies – removed the House of Bourbon from the throne of France once and for all. Louis-Philippe of the House of Orléans was then elected king but social ferment, general in Europe, led to the Revolution of 1848.

The resulting Second Republic was short lived. Through a *coup d'etat* in 1851 Napoleon III established the Second Empire. His imperial ambitions embroiled France in the Crimean War, war with Austria and an unsuccessful campaign in Mexico. In 1860 he annexed Nice and Savoy. But the story is not all of warmongering. Haussmann transformed Paris, with tree-lined boulevards sweeping away slums in the process, and ornamental parks were created, often on the site of old city walls and fortifications. Other cities followed suit, including Amiens and Lille. Queen Victoria came to Boulogne, en route to Paris to admire the new sights – the first British sovereign to visit the capital since the crowning of the infant Henry VI in 1422. Industry expanded, served by the new railways. Ostentatious new public buildings were erected, typified by the Beaux Arts Museums at Amiens and Lille. The Suez Canal was opened in 1869.

In 1870 came disaster. Napoleon III declared war on Prussia, and the North of France was to bear the brunt. At the Battle of Sedan the Emperor surrendered and was captured. Two days later the Third Republic was declared by Gambetta. The downfall of the Emperor was seized as an opportunity for a revolutionary uprising in Paris known as the Commune. The official retaliation was brutal and some 20,000 Communards were killed. Battles at Guise, St Quentin and Bapaume preceded the Prussian siege of Paris. The city, isolated from the rest of France, endured a bitter nineteen weeks of privation before falling to the enemy in January 1871. The defeat meant the humiliating loss for France of Alsace and Lorraine.

Whilst the period of the Third Republic was marked by some political instability, a new Constitution was created in 1875. The last quarter of the nineteenth century was a time of renewed prosperity – the period of the *belle époque*, and a degree of social reform. An alliance was signed with Russia in 1894 and the *entente cordiale* was concluded with England in 1904.

In 1914 tragedy struck again. Germany declared war on Russia, and in August attacked an ill-prepared France; and the Great War began, with offensives in Flanders and the Battle of the Marne. The Front extended from the coast near Dunkerque down to Switzerland. Bloody trench warfare ensued, with a particular concentration in the Amiens-Arras-Péronne triangle. The ultimate defeat of Germany by the Allies – England, France and, after November 1917, the Americans – was acknowledged by the Armistice of 11 November 1918. In a certain sense the nineteenth century ended in 1914 when the old Order disappeared. France was exhausted: her industries had been destroyed and the countryside of the North had been devastated. The human sacrifice of all the nations involved was enormous, but none suffered more than the French. Nearly 1.4 million Frenchmen were killed – one in five of the male population between the ages of twenty and forty-five.

The period between the First and Second World Wars was an unsettled time of political instability and economic crises in France, heightened by the world depression of 1929. The average age of the population continued to rise, exacerbated by the loss of men who would have fathered a new generation. Successive governments were weakened by the need to form coalitions with the Left and the Right. The 1930s were haunted by the rise of Fascism in Italy and Germany, while at home the increasing power of the Left led to the so-called Popular Front government of 1936.

In 1939, the English and, reluctantly, the French, declared war on Germany. As in 1914 France was insufficiently prepared. After the *Blitzkrieg* of May 1940 she was overrun by Germany in a mere five weeks, with devastating effect on the North of France. Marshal Pétain concluded an armistice with the victors, suspended the Third Republic, (created in the defeat of 1870), and set up his government at Vichy, whilst the Germans occupied the northern and western parts of France. This collaborationist move was soon undermined by the creation of an underground resistance movement (reinforced by the Communist Party after Germany attacked Russia in June 1941) and by the efforts of the young General de Gaulle, who had escaped to England with a number of servicemen, who became the forces of the Free French. By November 1942 the Vichy Government had collapsed, Germany occupied the whole of France, and a provisional government had been set up in Algiers under de Gaulle. The Germans were dominant in Europe from 1940 until 1942 but the tide began to turn after 1943 with heavy bombing of German cities and industry by the Allies.

On 6 June 1944 the British and Americans launched their offensive in Normandy. By August Paris had been relieved, but it took another year for the Germans to be finally routed. A peacetime government was formed under de Gaulle but he found it difficult to control a coalition of Communists, Socialists and Progressive Catholics, and resigned in 1946. The Fourth Republic was then inaugurated, under Vincent Auriol followed by René Coty.

Wartime bombing did not alter the landscape of the north to the same extent as in the First World War, but it did destroy the hearts of Dunkerque, Abbeville and Calais, and damage was considerable in Amiens, Boulogne and Arras. However, the severe depredations of the war on French industry led, with American aid, to a remarkable post-war rebuilding programme, and economic recovery.

The Common Market (EEC) was formed in 1957 by France, West Germany, Italy and the Benelux countries. But the 1950s was also a period of colonial unrest with the futile war in Indo-China and emergent nationalism in north and west Africa and Madagascar. Algeria was a particular problem with a million well-established French settlers reluctant to give in to the indigenous Muslim population. An army *coup d'état* in 1958 led to the return of de Gaulle, and the collapse of the Fourth Republic. The Fifth Republic initiated a new era of presidential power which lasted until the violent student riots in Paris and the general strike of May 1968.

Algerian independence was proclaimed in 1962 and large numbers of Algerians moved to French cities which created new social problems. De Gaulle resigned in 1969, after a referendum, to be succeeded by Georges Pompidou, who died in 1974. His successor, Valery Giscard d'Estaing was ousted by the swing to the left which brought in François Mitterand in 1981.

The 1980s has been a period of pragmatic rather than overt Socialism in France under Mitterand, and the power of the Communist Party has declined despite the initial popularity of the extreme right under Le Pen. President Mitterand was elected for a second term and seems destined to lead France into a new era when the Common Market countries remove their trade barriers in 1992, so creating a huge economic force in the world.

The post-war years in the North have seen a substantial decline in traditional industries such as textiles and coal-mining, with resulting pockets of high unemployment, the depopulation of the dense industrial areas and large-scale demolition, or transformation of nineteenth-century industrial buildings, such as has taken place in the North of England and South Wales. But there has been a vigorous investment in new industries such as car manufacture and electronics; fortunately these new developments have not swamped the traditional city centres and changed their character. However the advent of the Channel Tunnel, the construction of new motorways and the high-speed TGV railway will combine to make the North a new focal point in Western Europe. Already the North is in the path of new forms of invasion – with affluent English, Dutch and Germans seeking cheap holiday cottages and foreign developers buying up industrial and housing sites, but the one blessing is that the North is a huge area, still predominantly rural, the inhabitants are used to invasion, and their flexibility and capacity to absorb and adapt to outside influences suggest that Artois, Picardy and Flanders will remain as fascinating as ever to the traveller who takes the trouble to make the exploration.

ABBEVILLE: St Vulfran

ABBEVILLE: St Vulfran – medieval carved figure

ABBEVILLE: The château of Bagatelle

GAZETTEER

ABBEVILLE (Somme)

This very agreeable country town on the river Somme is the capital of the Ponthieu region of Picardy. Although 20 kms from the sea, it has been an inland port since ancient times, and, thanks to the wide canal, access by quite large boats is possible. Ecstatically praised, and sketched, by Ruskin, it was inhabited by quite a considerable English colony in the nineteenth century. The connection with England goes back to 1272, when Abbeville passed to the English crown on the marriage of Edward I and Eleanor of Castile, and it remained in English possession for two hundred years. In 1514 Mary Tudor, the sister of Henry VIII, celebrated her marriage here to Louis XII, and in 1527 Cardinal Wolsey signed an alliance with François I. In the First World War, Abbeville was an important English base serving the front line which George V and Queen Mary came to inspect.

The medieval heart of the town was destroyed in a single black day, 20 May 1940, by a heavy German air-raid intended to cow the inhabitants into submission, and part of a plan to cut off the British forces. It took many lives, destroyed many buildings and provoked the Picardy Resistance movement. This destruction was a great tragedy. Present day inhabitants still recall the horse-drawn cabs standing in a remarkably picturesque cobbled main square, enclosed by medieval houses and dominated by the great church of St Vulfran.

Today, this stately Flamboyant Gothic church, which was much admired by William Morris and Burne-Jones, still looms over the town centre but, half a century since the bombardment, remains encased in scaffolding for seemingly indefinite restoration. Visits are possible, but only on Tuesdays in summer at 2 pm. The guided tour includes a precipitate climb up to the roof for splendid views over the townscape and the surrounding countryside. If this is not possible one can at least admire the splendid Renaissance carved oak main doors of 1550, and the profusion of sculpture of religious figures, particularly those above the right hand portal which are less worn. Around the corner, in the rue du Pomme d'Amour, high up in an angle of the building, is a very rude figure indeed.

Inside, the splendid height of the nave is emphasized by its narrowness and by the strong vertical lines of the ribs, unbroken by capitals, soaring from the floor up to the vaulting thirty metres above. The interior is still bare of furnishings and the main interest is the expressive sculpture of the reredos in the aisle chapels — a Last Judgement is particularly entertaining. The church was restored in the nineteenth century by Viollet-le-Duc; he created an *arc-de-triomphe* over the main portal which is a successful embellishment. The choir was not completed until the seventeenth century, in a very ugly late Gothic style, redeemed, if that is the word, by some brilliantly-coloured post-war stained glass by an American artist, William Einstein, a serving soldier who remained after the war to marry a Picarde. The glass, in strong primary colours, is said not to be abstract, but it is not easy to discern the representation.

The townscape surrounding St Vulfran is fairly typical of post-war rebuilding but it does have a certain coherence and style and a sympathetic street pattern, with, thankfully, no destructive inner ring roads. Somewhere hereabouts the writer Fenimore Cooper enjoyed "a marvellously cooked dinner of game". In the centre, the clean lines of the Hôtel de Ville, with its tall slim belfry tower, has something of the panache of 1930s Scandinavian civic architecture, although it was actually built in 1960. In the lobby is a remarkable list of all the mayors since 1184, when the town gained its civic freedom.

Despite the wanton German destruction, much old architecture can still be seen. At No 1 place Clemenceau is a lonely survivor of the medieval gabled houses which once filled the town while handsome late seventeenth- and eighteenth-century town mansions recall the prosperity created by the establishment of fine quality textile manufacturing, notably by the van Robais family who came here from Holland in 1685, at the instigation of that imaginative politician Colbert (this was one of his many schemes to create new industries in France). The van Robais later built, in 1752, an enchanting folly of a house, Bagatelle, secluded in a small park on the southern outskirts of the town. The de Wailly family, who have been there since 1810, allow visits and the opportunity should certainly be taken, thus following in the footsteps of the composers Erik Satie and Vincent d'Indy, who were often entertained at Bagatelle. This small and desirable Louis XV *pavillon* has an intimate Rococo interior with an ingenious staircase curving up in two flights – an object lesson of grandeur in miniature. One room has an early example of Pompeian decoration in France. The architect is not known – Gabriel has been suggested – but its late Baroque exterior indicates a provincial designer. A small museum devoted to the Second World War, is housed in one of the flanking wings, which, although in keeping date only from the early years of this century.

Since Abbeville is contained in a compact oval, ringed by boulevards, and is only a mile across at its widest, it is easily explored by foot in a morning. To the west is the 1912 Flemish-Gothic railway station – a surprising survivor of the bombing, and now a classified monument, at the end of a cul-de-sac with cafés of some character with 1920s lettering. Nearby, adjoining the canal bridge,

is a curious 1907 Memorial with a macabre panel by Raoul Delhomme; it was 'erected by the proletariat', to commemorate the execution in 1766 of a nineteen-year-old aristocrat, the Chevalier de la Barre, for mutilating a crucifix. The event was actually a *cause célèbre* at the time of his execution and was denounced by radicals such as Voltaire. In the early 1900s there was a strong anticlerical movement in France – hence this monument.

To the north of the Hôtel de Ville, and partly housed in ancient buildings which include the Belfry of 1209 – reputedly the oldest in France – the Musée de Boucher de Perthes has a good collection of medieval wood carvings, in particular a rich polychrome altarpiece depicting the life of the Virgin; paintings, including some allegorical works by Lemoyne; local Vron and Sorrus pottery; and a large collection of palaeontology (assembled by Boucher de Perthes, one of the creators of this science – he is commemorated by a monument by Nadaud in the town cemetery).

The large square adjoining, the place Amiral Courbet, contains an ornate and rather war-battered monument to the Admiral by Falguière. The *quartier* to the north of the square has some old winding streets, with weatherboarded houses here and there and one or two survivors of the medieval houses which excited John Ruskin, such as that at No 29 rue des Capucins. Nearby is a nineteenth-century butcher's shop; by contrast, to the south, is a jolly Art Deco blue-tiled butcher's at No 11 place du Pont Neuf. At No 26 rue le Sueur, now the Chamber of Commerce, there is a good example of eighteenth-century architecture, the noble gateway of which boasts sculpture of high quality. In the same street, the Banque de France is housed in one of the few remaining town mansions set in its own grounds.

Cross the river for a view of the quays, and enter the Chaussée d'Hocques to see the factory built by the van Robais in 1709; known as the Manufacture des Rames, with

ABBEVILLE: Eighteenth century doorway

MERS-LES-BAINS: Fin-de-siècle houses

its splendid gateway carved with putti, it is a rare and important example of early industrial architecture, which will eventually become a museum.

South from the Hôtel de Ville, something of the aristocratic past of the town is to be found in the rue du Maréchal Foch, with very fine eighteenth-century gateways at No 58 (derelict alas) and No 60, and further along, in the rue St Gilles, at No 19 and No 21 (by Pfaff – see entry for Valloires). In a side street, rue du Pont de Boulogne, at No 4, is another medieval survivor, with carved heads, perhaps actual portraits, with rather sinister half-smiles on their faces. Now a hospital, No 20 rue Millevoye has a particularly fine early eighteenth-century gateway of intricately carved stone. On a lighter note, opposite the busy modern hospital in the avenue du Rivage is a café waggishly entitled 'Mieux ici qu'en face'! The main street eastwards from the Hôtel de Ville, the rue Chaussée du Bois, passes the ruined Baroque facade of the chapel of the Couvent des Ursulines, standing like a theatre backdrop, and leads to the large war memorial by Chabaut on the main roundabout, which is worth a glance now that it has been cleaned and the detail is clearly visible. In the avenue du Général Leclerc, the main road leading south-east from the roundabout, the new building housing the gendarmerie is a striking piece of modern architecture.

Abbeville: South-West Excursion

An excursion along the Le Treport road (D925) into the region known as the Vimeu takes in **Miannay**, where there is a stylish church built in 1962, with a tall, detached campanile and interesting stained glass. At **Moyenneville** one can enjoy from the gateway, a large 1880s model-farm complex in brick, flint and half-timbering, worthy of the Rothschilds at Waddesdon.

Further west, the villages of **Friville-**

Escarbotin and **Fressenville** are centres for lock-making; craftwork in brass, ormolu and gunmetal is still an important industry in France and a worthwhile museum has been opened in an attractive old building at Friville, the Musée des Industries du Vimeu. An evocative panel on the 1914–18 war memorial in Friville, which depicts a dying soldier with mourning figures, set against a symbolically setting sun – is the work of Albert Roze, a sculptor from Amiens with a prolific output in the region.

Continue towards **Le Tréport**. This delightful small port, with its Art Nouveau resort, **Mers-les-Bains**, – which has recently been declared a *secteur sauvegardé* – a conservation area of architectural interest – and its historic neighbouring town of **Eu**, well-known to Queen Victoria, are over the border in Normandy; they are full of interest, but beyond the scope of this book. Turn west along the D19 to the sea, reached rather suddenly at **Ault-Onival**. This late nineteenth-century resort town remains largely unchanged and retains its *petit-bourgeois* atmosphere. There are excellent views of the cliffs of Le Tréport, which have been a favourite subject for many artists, including Cotman, Delacroix and Corot. Local ceramics works were kept busy supplying colourful pictorial tile panels, and there are innumerable name plaques to be seen on retirement and holiday houses such as 'Doux-Nid' and 'Mon Rêve'. The fourteenth-century church of St Pierre built of stone, with chequer patterns of flint and pebbles, is handsome enough; outside is the war memorial, an erect figure of a soldier and rather English in its style. Opposite, the post office is decorated with ceramic plaques depicting postage stamps of the 1920s; inside are period tiled floors, which are becoming rare these days and fast disappearing under the ubiquitous pvc. The Villa Mama, on the hill out of town, has a particular Art Nouveau flavour.

Just along the coast is the more prosperous small resort of **Le Bois-de-Cise**. A narrow thickly-wooded valley slopes steeply down to the minute pebble beach, again with good cliff views. Dotted among the trees are *fin de siècle* villas with ceramic name plaques such as 'Les Chardons d'Ecosse', while others may recall mistresses installed by Parisian businessmen – 'Villa Yvonne', 'Beatrice', 'Cizette', 'Chalet Marie-Pierre'. It is a rare place in which to evoke the era of Proustian resorts.

Abbeville: North Excursion

Take the N1 north from Abbeville and then the D105 into the region known as the Ponthieu, through the 4,500 hectare oak and beech forest of Crécy, the home of deer and wild boar, to the pleasing small town of **Crécy-en-Ponthieu**, which has a handsome medieval church with a distinctive tower and, in its centre, an odd monument of brick with reused ancient carved capitals. A plaque in both French and English proclaims that it was erected by Eleanor of Aquitaine, who was also Countess of Ponthieu, in thanks for the return of her sons, Richard the Lionheart and John Lackland, from the Crusades. Nearby is another monument, erected in 1905, and an early anticipation of the Art Deco style, to the brave and blind king of Bohemia whose emblem, a black shield with plumes, was reputedly assumed by the Prince of Wales. There is another monument to the same king on the D56 road to Fontaine-sur-Maye: a battered cross on a plinth, on the spot where he fell, which is perhaps the oldest war memorial in northern France.

Just to the east, between the D111 and the D938, is the site of the famous battle of 1346, when Edward III defeated a much larger French army, thanks mainly to the proficiency of his English archers. 20,000 men at arms, 1,300 French knights and eleven princes perished in the mud at Crécy, and it marked the beginning of the Hundred Years War. On the site of the windmill used by Edward III as a look-out post is a modern timber viewing platform, a hideous new car park, and a panel which describes the scale

BRAILLY: The château

CRÉCY: Monument to the King of Bohemia

ST RIQUIER: The belfry

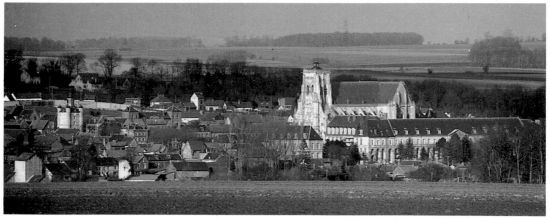

ST RIQUIER: View from the south

of the slaughter – to be repeated five centuries later at the Battle of the Somme. It is all very didactic and typically French.

The D56 leads south-east to **Brailly**. Within the confines of the village stands the eighteenth-century château of Brailly-Cornehotte. Its fine classical facade, enriched with carved panels, and its formal garden with topiary, can be easily appreciated through the decorative wrought-iron gateway. From Brailly, turn south to reach **St Riquier** from the north. This is the best approach to this town and ensures that all its visual pleasures unroll in the best sequence, beginning with the view down its steep main street, with the distinctive sixteenth-century belfry tower on the right, and the great square tower of the abbey on the left. Straight ahead is the tiny Maison Petit, its tricorn-shaped roof reflecting the profession of its first owner – a soldier in Napoleon's *Grande Armée*. This cheerful little house possesses a vital element of humour, in contrast to the might of church and state. Do not miss, on the right at the top of the hill, the Hôtel Dieu – a hospital, built in 1719, with a characteristic horseshoe-shaped entrance stairway echoed by the curved portal. The interior has work by Pfaff and Parrocel – see the entry for Valloires.

The major architectural feature of the town is the splendid mainly sixteenth-century Benedictine abbey church, a very early foundation of 640. The massive Flamboyant Gothic tower has an abundance of good sculpture. The eighteenth-century additions are extensive, housing a museum devoted to the rural life of Picardy.

On entering the church one is immediately struck by the wonderful luminosity of the white stone and the exquisite lines of the architecture. Below the characteristic eighteenth-century organ are sculpted figures of St Christopher and St James on intricately carved bases – reminders that the church was a stage on one of the pilgrim routes to St James of Compostella in Spain. The interior is well-endowed with sculpture and paintings,

notably the sixteenth-century murals in the treasury. The choir has an accomplished wrought-iron screen and carved stalls; as in Amiens Cathedral these form an eighteenth-century enclave, counterpointing the Gothic. In the right hand aisle is a stone sculpture of Joan of Arc, who was imprisoned in the town in 1430 on her way to Rouen and the stake. Its style is Gothic, though it dates only from 1930 – anachronistic but highly effective. To appreciate the dramatic skyline formed by the abbey and belfry, riding high above the roof tops of the town, take the D183 south from St Riquier.

AIRE-SUR-LA-LYS (Pas-de-Calais)

Aire is one of the most attractive towns in a prosperous farming area, watered by several rivers, where Flanders meets Artois. In the Grand'Place, the handsome stone Hôtel de Ville of 1717, by Héroguelle, a pupil of Hardouin-Mansart, is flanked by pilastered eighteenth-century houses and a tall belfry tower with a cheerful carillon, which plays popular airs every quarter-hour. On the south side of the Place is the elegant Flemish Renaissance bailliage or bailiwick – now the tourist office – with sculpted friezes representing the Virtues and The Four Elements, which were originally painted and gilded. To the north is the chapel of St Jacques (1682) in the characteristically vigorous Jesuit Baroque style. The enormous and splendid

AIRE-SUR-LA-LYS: The Hôtel de Ville

Flamboyant Gothic church – the Collégiale St Pierre – has a 62 metre tower which would not be out of place in Somerset. But look closely, for the classical details betray the repair necessary after a siege in 1710. The vast interior, 104 metres long and 38 metres wide, has a majestic seventeenth-century organ. The annual festival procession features the Scottish princess Crymhilde who, according to legend, married the local hero Lyderic and founded Aire, Ghent and Lille; both are represented as giants. It also celebrates the *andouille*, the local sausage speciality.

Aire-sur-la-Lys: Excursion

From Aire take the D943, and then the D916 to **Hazebrouck**, an important base for Wellington's forces in 1815, and a major rail junction for British troops in the Great War. En route is **Morbecque**, which has a pretty seventeenth-century Hôtel de Ville of brick with stone dressings and a well restored church with indifferent modern stained glass. The war memorial at the gateway, depicting a dying soldier, is an effective sculpture by Jules Déchin of 1920. Although ignored by Michelin, Hazebrouck, a textile town and the capital of the Houtland, looks promising when approached from the south. From some distance away, the great pinnacled church tower, reminiscent of churches in Somerset, can be seen rising from the plain, framed by the roadside trees. The sixteenth-century three-naved *hallekerke* church of St Eloi is built of mellow rose brick with stone dressings, and has been sympathetically restored. The brick and stone mixture is echoed inside, complemented by good eighteenth-century gilded ironwork, a relatively tame gilded baldachino, and some rather somber 1920s glass in murky colours. The nearby war memorial, by Desruelles, in gleaming white stone, is of the implacable Marianne, the emblem of Republican France, her hands at rest on the pommel of her sword, which is symbolically entwined with foliage.

The town's main square is a big and generous space, dominated by the stately neo-classical Hôtel de Ville of 1807–20 by Drapier, with a broad colonnaded and arcaded stone facade. Around the square is a good variety of shops and houses some with old-fashioned lettering such as that found at Au Petit Paris; in the south-east corner, a sports-car is a dashing motif on a 1930s facade. Set away from the square is a former Augustine convent dating from the seventeenth-century, though its authentic-looking tall and handsome Flemish Baroque gables were actually constructed in 1895. The windows on the north elevation are decorated at eye level with carved masks – powerful grotesques with definitely heathen characteristics which are somewhat at variance with the views, and vows, of its former inmates. It now houses the Musée Municipal, recently improved and worth a visit, which contains a recreated traditional Flemish kitchen, Dutch and Flemish school pictures and paintings of the nineteenth century, which include a lively portrait of the artist Georges Clairin, the lifelong companion of the actress Sarah Bernhardt. This is a good town for a quick walkabout, with some unusual shop details, such as the 1930s stained glass Negro heads above the Deux Nègres shoe shop. On the outskirts of the town, the church of Notre Dame is an impressive postwar building and a tribute to the craft of the bricklayer; it is quite severe, with a very tall campanile, and has sculpture in the porch by Coetlogon. To the south, the D946 leads to the forest of Nieppe, the largest expanse of woodland in Flanders. Here, British cavalry charges actually halted the German advance in October 1914. **La Motte au Bois**, a hamlet within the forest, has atmosphere. There is a seventeenth-century château nearby, and a church built in 1680 and moved stone by stone from Aire-sur-la-Lys in 1928. On the southern edge of the forest, the small industrial town of **Merville**, on the River Lys, was completely destroyed in the Great War. It must have done well out of war reparation to have afforded such a lavish Hôtel de Ville, a characteristic design by Louis Cordonnier. Its splendid belfry looms above an immense square with a bandstand; in the distance can be seen Cordonnier's church of St Pierre with its twin towers – also on a grand scale. The town of **Estaires**, 6 kms due east, another town destroyed in the Great War, is also on the Lys; despite its small size, it boasts an enormous neo-Flemish Hôtel de Ville, built in a rather fierce red brick. The nearby church of St Vaast is conventional and dull, but the white stone spire is elegant, and there is sculpture over the main portal by R. Coin. The war memorial nearby, unsigned, but in the style of Desruelles, of a female figure holding a wreath aloft, has excellent lettering at its base – 'A nos morts'.

A short detour should be taken to **Lestrem**, 4 kms to the south-west by the D945, where the handsome sixteenth-century church of St Amé, painstakingly rebuilt after mining by the Germans in the Great War, contains excellent stained glass by Magne, and statues, stations of the cross and reredos by Bouchard. The reredos are a reduced version of those at Arras Cathedral.

AMIENS (Somme)

Amiens is the capital of Picardy, strategically sited on the great River Somme, and set in the heart of the vast rural expanse of the North of France. The industry of Lille is almost as distant as Paris.

As the city was behind the British lines in the Great War, it was a haven for dinner and entertainment, away from the turmoil of the Front. It also saw perhaps one of the greatest concentrations of prostitutes in the history of warfare. Sir William Orpen was here as a war artist, and castigated its depravity in his vivid account of his war experiences in France published in 1921. These days it has a sombre air and lacks a Grand'Place to provide its citizens with a focal point with all the bustle of café life, and its infuriating one-way system seems designed to prevent a tour of the sights by car.

The city is dominated by one of the glories of the North, the Cathedral of Notre Dame standing high above the river, the largest Gothic church in France and one of the pinnacles of medieval architecture. It was constructed to the designs of Robert of Luzarches between 1220 and 1260 – a comparatively short period for such an immense undertaking resulting in a unified and harmonious building. William Morris, was inspired by the cathedral to take up the study of architecture, after visiting it as a student with Burne-Jones in 1855. He wrote "I think I felt inclined to shout when I first entered Amiens Cathedral; it is so free and vast and noble ..." They both resolved at the end of their walking tour to give up theology and devote their lives to art and architecture. J.L. Pearson, the architect of numerous Gothic Revival churches in England, was another Englishman to be stimulated by his visit.

For Eugène Viollet-le-Duc, its restorer in the nineteenth century (and the 'medieva-liser' of the château of Pierrefonds and the walled city of Carcassonne), it was 'the perfect Gothic church'. Inevitably he could not resist tampering with its perfection: interposing the top-most gallery between the towers on the west facade. Viollet-le-Duc had a profound influence on English Gothic Revival architects such as William Burges and indeed on the later French Art Nouveau movement. It is significant that William Morris would have seen, in its pristine state, the vividly coloured neo-medieval decoration of Viollet-le-Duc's chapel in the apse, recently completed to commemorate the visit of the Emperor.

On the west front is a vivid anthology of medieval sculpture which inspired John Ruskin to write his *Bible of Amiens*, later translated by Marcel Proust. Ruskin's aim was to point out that the sculpture was conceived to educate the illiterate faithful. The central porch is dominated by a serene figure of Christ, known as the Beau Dieu, flanked by the Apostles, the prophets and the wise and foolish Virgins. High up, below the rose window, is a gallery of colossal figures of twenty-two kings. The sculpture of the south door is also remarkable, and includes the famous gilded Virgin.

Surprisingly, the majestic interior is bathed in light, in sharp contrast to the dark and mysterious interior of Notre Dame in Paris. This is some recompense for the tragic loss of the medieval stained glass. Cross the wide uncluttered nave to reach the choir, pausing to examine the tombs of the founder bishops, Evrard de Fouilloy and Geoffroy d'Eu, on either side – rare examples in France of early bronze funerary monuments. The nave is paved in intricate patterns, difficult to appreciate properly except from above. At the crossing turn your eyes to admire the intricate tracery of the marvellous rose windows. In the north and south transepts, on either side of the steps to the choir, are two fine classical altars of 1625–35 by the Amienois Nicholas Blasset which are very sophisticated for their date. The eighteenth century has left its unmistakable and elegant marks on the choir, with Baroque altars by Dupuis and an outstanding Louis XV ironwork screen, sumptuously gilded and forged by Jean Weyren of Corbie, who also worked at the abbey of Valloires. The ambulatory aisles, both north and south, have striking medieval polychrome sculptured scenic groups, evoking the life of St Firmin (south aisle) and the life of St John (north aisle). It is essential to get permission to enter the choir in order to appreciate a major work of sixteenth-century art: the 110 stalls, prodigiously carved in oak, depict some 3,600 figures in early Renaissance dress, not only enacting scenes from the Old and New Testaments but engaged also in local activities, an invaluable document of medieval life.

Some medieval glass survives in the apse, together with, by contrast, good 1920s glass by Jean Gaudin of Paris. The monument and tomb of Canon Lucas is another excellent work by Blasset and features the popular statue of the weeping cherub. There are several memorials commemorating British and Commonwealth soldiers who fell in the Battle of the Somme, including Raymond Asquith, the elder son of the Prime Minister, whose loss was keenly felt by his circle, which included Winston Churchill. The 1914–18 war memorial to the parishioners, is by Albert Roze, a good sculptor active in the region after the Great War.

West of the cathedral, much of the city was laid waste in 1940, and has been blandly rebuilt, the occasional old building usually over-restored.

Taking the rue Dusevel, one passes the popular bronze sculpture of Marie Sans Chemise – a sweet naked maiden symbolising 'Spring', by Albert Roze, which used to adorn the town clock until it was damaged in the last war – and reaches the town centre and the bulky Hôtel de Ville, now cleaned to reveal stonework of a beautiful colour. The Peace of Amiens was signed here in 1802, marking a lull in the hostilities between France and England – depicted in a large painting by Ziegler (1853) on view on the first floor, which features the signatories, Napoleon and Cornwallis. The lull allowed Wordsworth to visit France to see for the first time, his nine-year old love child, the fruit of a youthful affair with Annette Vallon. The Hôtel de Ville incidentally stands on the site of a gigantic Roman amphitheatre which seated 13,000 spectators. Nearby is the bailliage (also known as La Malmaison), an elegant building of 1541, a late flowering of the Flamboyant Gothic style, but the well-sculpted portrait busts on its facade reveal the new Renaissance influence. To the north is the market place, where stands the old belfry, built in 1408; in 1940 it lost its eighteenth-century tower but this is being restored. Now in view is the Flamboyant Gothic church of St Germain-l'Ecossais, with its leaning tower. In the nearby place au Feurre, a small eighteenth century stone house incorporates a handsome fountain with a bronze mask set in an arched niche

AMIENS: The cathedral

AMIENS: The gilded Virgin

AMIENS: The church of St Honoré

24

with vermiculated rustication, one of the pleasing events in this war-ravaged area. To the west is all that remains of the cloister of the Soeurs Grises, a handsome Doric screen wall which has all its detail turned inwards, looking like stage scenery. Nearby, at No 3 rue de Condé, the Centre d'Exposition du Costume, a private costume museum, is housed in a pretty eighteenth-century house, a rare survivor of the 1940 bombardment and a visit is highly recommended for its intact and unspoilt interior – with panelling, wrought-iron staircase and chimney-pieces of the period – enhanced by an erudite guided tour of the exquisite collection of period costume. At the north end of this street, passing what looks like the outer wall of a Victorian prison, a recently restored eighteenth-century pavilion with canted corners and a balustrade below a small belvedere, is the elegant office of the local water company, aptly embellished with a fountain. Southwards, close to the two rather dull churches of St Jacques and the Temple, is a tall eighteenth-century house with extensive vermiculated decoration and a good Rococo bronze Neptune fountain, again set in an arched niche. At the west end of the adjacent rue Jean Catelas, the excellent 1947 building and its landscaping, is by Pierre Dufau and will one day be appreciated as a period piece. Behind the Maison de la Culture in the place Léon Gontier – the first such institution to be opened in France, designed by Pierre Sonrel in 1965 and a good example of its kind – is the Hôtel Stengel, a former eighteenth-century cavalry barracks with carved military trophies.

In the rue Frédéric Petit, the University of Amiens occupies the former abbey of the Prémontrés St Jean. Far from being an ancient monastic pile, as its name might suggest, this is an excellent eighteenth-century town building around a courtyard, with good wrought-iron work and a sculpted pediment by a local man, Cressent. Now that it has been so miraculously restored, it is difficult to believe that it was ruined in the last war. The nineteenth-century ceramics on the facade of a house opposite merit a glance. The big 1914–18 war memorial at the end of the street, in the Place Maréchal Foch, is an undistinguished work by Roze. Turning the corner into the rue Desprez, the Ecole des Beaux Arts et de Musique is a late work of Louis Duthoit, its completion in 1931 coinciding with his death. the sculptress Anne-Marie Roux and stained-glass maker Jean Gaudin contributed to the decoration. Compared with his Hôtel Bouctôt (see below), Duthoit was less at home with the Art Deco style, but this building is rewarding enough with typical ironwork, sculpted panels, lettering, stained glass and – something of an oddity – a heavy bulk of stone figures sitting incongruously on a modern glass roof-light. To the south, across the busy boulevard Carnot, is the curious church of St Honoré, built after the last war but actually a replica – but with modifications imposed by the diocese – of the Papal Pavilion by Paul Tournon, erected for the 1937 Paris International Exhibition. He was the architect of two even more unusual churches which were part of Cardinal Verdier's ambitious building programme in Paris in the 1930s, as well as the Sacré Coeur, Casablanca.

The facade has striking brick sculpture by Florence Tournon, the wife of the architect, and inside there is some excellent stained glass by Archepel in the soaring central lantern. Along the boulevard to the east is another curiosity, and a rarity: the Cirque Municipal, by Emile Ricquier, a permanent structure for entertainment, seating 3,000 people, which was inaugurated in 1889 by Jules Verne, who had settled in the city and became a local councillor and a prominent citizen. He is commemorated by a sculpture by Albert Roze, located to the east in the park just to the south of the boulevard, here called mail Albert I. His bust stands on an Art Nouveau column of 1908; a group of figures in front are clearly taking pleasure in reading his works. Close by, No 2 rue Charles Dubois, one of his several homes in the city, has become a centre for the study of his life and works. The courtyard has *fin-de-siècle* tiling and a large *marquise* – a glazed canopy.

Across the boulevard, towards the city centre, in the rue de la République, the Musée de Picardie is an essential visit. This proud Second Empire building was designed 1855–67 by A.S. Diet as a palace of art in the wake of the new Louvre. The outstanding murals by Puvis de Chavannes – who inspired Gauguin and Seurat among others – provided the model for a prolific output of mural painting in official buildings in Edwardian England. The energies of the local association of antique dealers raised the funds for the construction.

Given the proximity of the Low Countries it is inevitable that the collections should have a preponderance of Flemish, Spanish and Dutch paintings, but the most notable pictures are French eighteenth-century: these include the self portrait of Maurice Quentin de la Tour, hunting scenes formerly at Versailles, and 'The Laundresses' by Fragonard. The nineteenth-century collection features works by Delacroix and Géricault, while the twentieth century is represented by Bonnard and Matisse. There is also a collection, unique to Amiens, of late medieval paintings with splendid carved Gothic frames, glorifying the Virgin. These are the survivors of annual commissions by a local religious society, the Confrérie du Puy Notre Dame d'Amiens.

Improvements are in progress and new galleries have been created in the basement, devoted to prehistory and demonstrating the importance of Amiens as a Roman city – Samarobriva.

The former chapel of the building now incongruously houses the museum café, with its lavish neo-medieval decorative scheme in blue and gold recently restored. Adjoining the museum is the Bibliothèque, a fine neo-Classical building (1826) with a colonnade, built E-shaped around a spacious forecourt. Opposite the museum, the Hôtel du Préfet, a handsome neo-Classical mansion of 1773

by Montigny, is the seat of the administrator of the region. To the north, still in the rue de la République, is the former Caisse d'Epargne, recently cleaned – revealing the details of the pediment sculpture by Albert Roze. Now turn into the rue des Jacobins, which has a number of post Great War flourishes in the Art Deco style, including the huge Palais de l'Auto, now more prosaically the local Renault garage. Just off to the north, in the rue Marotte, is a good surviving building of 1893: a galleried interior can be glimpsed through the iron grille of the main door. To the south in the rue des Otages, the Chambre Régionale de Commerce is housed in the grand 1908 Hôtel Bouctôt-Wagniez. Gothic blended with Art Nouveau, designed by Louis Duthoit; his artist brother, Adrien Duthoit, collaborated with him on the astonishing and rich interior, which retains its luxurious *belle époque* furnishings, stained-glass and wrought-iron work. This important work of the period is surprisingly little known, even to the locals.

To the east the skyscraper opposite the station, the Tour Perret, is a late work (1952) by Auguste Perret, who planned the rebuilding of Le Havre. It is principally remarkable for its height of 104 metres, and at the time it was the tallest modern building in Europe. One can imagine the fuss if such a tower had been suggested in an English cathedral city: here it obtrudes without offending, probably because its relatively slim profile conforms to a long tradition of tall urban towers. The large adjoining square and the main station, are also by Perret and form a reasonably success-ful piece of post-war town planning, grand in layout if a little bland in execution. The city has recently commissioned a distinguished town-planner, Rob Krier of Vienna, to pre-pare a master-plan for the town centre; it is likely to be a sensitive scheme, and if executed, of great benefit to Amiens. Nearby, in the rue Lamartine, the small and com-fortable hotel, the Normandie can be recom-mended for its attractive 1930s stained glass.

Heading back towards the centre, in the place René Goblet, is a poor post World War Two monument by Jan and Joel Martel, unworthy of the local hero, Marshal Leclerc. To the west, in the rue des Trois Cailloux, is the elegant neo-Classical stone facade of the former Théâtre (1780) by Jacques Rousseau, now a bank, with excellent thematic sculpture. To the north is the big classical pile of the Palais de Justice, and nearby a picturesque group is formed by the sixteenth-century Maison du Sagittaire and the Logis du Roi – the onetime headquarters of a local literary society, the Rosati, an anagram of Artois.

It is easy to miss the Hôtel de Berny – the Musée d'Art Local et d'Histoire Régionale – which is screened by a high wall, in the rue Victor Hugo. This splendid Louis XIII mansion, of brick with a profusion of stone rustication, is set in a charming garden planted *à la française*, with a pretty pavilion. It provides an ideal setting for a very enjoyable decorative arts collection, assembled with great refinement by a local senator, Gérard de Berny. The furniture, pictures and imported panelling, mainly of the seventeenth and eighteenth centuries, are of high quality. There is a portrait of Choderlos de Laclos, who was born in Amiens and is best known for his controversial erotic novel *Les Liaisons Dangereuses*.

The quality of presentation beautifully illustrates the argument for showing decorative arts in a domestic setting rather than in a purpose built museum. Upstairs is a contribution from the twentieth-century: a showcase of ceramics from the local Moutières factory, which produced colourful work in the Art Nouveau and Art Deco styles between 1917 and 1939. At No 40 rue Victor Hugo the *atelier* of Claude Barre contains a very interesting small museum of stained glass (visits only at 3 pm). This is an opportunity to examine the medium at close quarters and visit one of the old town houses.

The cathedral is now close at hand, and the *quartier* to its east has a number of good town houses of the seventeenth and eighteenth centuries, such as those in the rue Metz l'Evêque and the rue des Augustins, both of which lead down to the river.

Cross to the north bank for a good view of the cathedral and to enter the *quartier* St Leu, an area redolent of Holland with its canal-side cottages, early gabled houses and old mills. The tight-knit community was an early industrial zone devoted to textile production. Amiens has for centuries been noted for the manufacture of velvet, but it is now produced in the new industrial estates in the suburbs. There are still cast-iron stand-pipes in the streets but, alas, the *quartier* is beginning to be tarted up and developed in a chi-chi fashion. To the east of St Leu are the *hortillonages* – rich silty market gardens, watered by tributaries of the Somme, which are only accessible by boat and can be visited in spring and summer.

On the south-east outskirts of the city, the cemetery in the suburb of St Acheul contains a touching war memorial by Roze and train enthusiasts will head onwards to the extensive railway yards at **Longueau** where impressive engine-sheds curve around the turntables. In the 1970s, Longueau was the last bastion of the steam age in France.

Another local excursion should be made to the north-west of the city. The N1 passes a network of formal canals enclosing the Jardin des Plantes, and soon reaches the Citadelle, an example of early seventeenth-century military architecture by Errard de Bar-le-Duc which anticipated the work of Vauban. The D191 leads westwards to the atmospheric garden-cemetery of the Madeleine, a bosky museum of funerary art inaugurated in 1817, where the bizarre tomb of Jules Verne may be found – a torso bursting out of the ground in anticipation of resurrection, one arm outstretched to the sky. It is by the ubiquitous sculptor, Albert Roze, who was responsible for many other monuments in the cemetery.

THE SOMME: *View of the river*

VILLERS–BRETONNEUX: *The view from Lutyens's Australian memorial*

Amiens-East Excursion:
The Battlefields of the Somme

A tour of the Somme, with its battlefields, cemeteries and memorials, is an essential part of any visit to the North of France. Now that the events of 1916 will soon be beyond living memory, the battlefields themselves have acquired an added dimension, silent witnesses to the catastrophic events that today seem difficult to comprehend.

The rolling landscape of the Somme is wide, varied and attractive, its openness a permanent reminder of the devastation of the countryside by one of the fiercest conflicts in history. The Front is characterised by huge horizons dotted with church towers and silos, pockets of woodland along the Somme and Ancre rivers, and the virtual absence of any buildings that predate the 1920s; its most striking features are the innumerable cemeteries, mostly British, dotted all over the landscape, sometimes small and intimate, sometimes on a scale that is truly monumental. It would be too difficult to visit all the cemeteries, since there are 918 in all, and many are, in any case, of limited interest in visual terms, though all are powerful reminders. This selection therefore concentrates on those which are the most striking architecturally, or which feature sculptural decoration.

The Great War, which marked a watershed in Western Civilisation, was the first to involve the whole nation and the first to create a widespread desire for permanent remembrance.

In 1918, the Imperial War Graves Commission, which came into being largely through the energies of Fabian Ware, appointed the leading architects of the day for this vast undertaking: Sir Edwin Lutyens, Herbert Baker and Reginald Blomfield, both later knighted. A team under their leadership produced a standard concept for the smaller cemeteries, which was adapted with great ingenuity to suit the particularities of each site and its setting in the landscape. They were built to a very high standard, using the best materials and with imaginative planting, and are still impeccably maintained by the Commission (now called the Commonwealth War Graves Commission). A monumental and severe Classicism, which eschewed sentimental sculpture, was the style adopted, and was intended to convey a sense of permanent memorial. There was initially much debate and controversy over the numerous issues involved, which included the question of whether the Christian symbol of the Cross should be used. This was actively promoted by Baker, but opposed by Lutyens, partly on the grounds that many non-Christians had participated in the war. Baker was keen on sentiment, whilst Lutyens and Blomfield wanted the designs to be monumental and abstract. Indeed Blomfield advised the junior architects to take as a model for their inspiration, the severity of the work of Vauban. Lutyens wanted no celebration of victory or glorification with cannons. In the event a compromise was reached. The Great War Stone, a monolith designed by Lutyens, with the inscription 'Their name liveth for evermore', and the Cross of Sacrifice, designed by Blomfield, featured in almost all the cemeteries, though in some a Cross by Lutyens was erected. One important feature was that no distinction was to be made between officers and men; all headstones were to be of the same form.

For many the trauma of the war hung like a black cloud over the nineteen-twenties. Vaughan Williams' experiences as an ambulance driver in France inspired his remote and mystical Third Symphony. There was an enormous output of poetry. Wilfred Owen, Siegfried Sassoon, Robert Graves and Edmund Blunden were among the British poets who fought at the Front and evoked their experience in verse. The awesome task of identifying the dead in the aftermath of the war was very well portrayed by Bertrand Tavernier in his sombre 1989 film 'La vie et rien d'autre'.

Take the D1 east from Amiens to **Daours**. The Military Cemetery, with its pair of brick, stone and pantiled loggias and grove of fruit trees, was designed by Lutyens. Almost opposite, a narrow road follows the north bank of the Somme (a back road to Corbie) and leads to Corbie Military Cemetery. This is one of the few cemeteries to have been designed by Dr Charles Holden (appointed additional Principal Architect in France in 1920 but who declined a knighthood), the architect best known for his later work, such as the Senate House at London University and *avant garde* tube stations for London Transport. Set in a field and screened from the river by poplars, the graves are guarded by two plain stone cenotaphs, as severe as block-houses but with subtle detailing.

Continue into **La Neuville**, on the way to Corbie, and you will pass a little church, Notre Dame de l'Assomption, the portal of which is decorated with a very lively sixteenth-century bas-relief showing Christ's entry into Jerusalem on Palm Sunday. An astonishing survival considering its location close to the Front, it is similar to the sculpture at Mailly-Maillet to the north, and is full of entertaining details, including some figures who have climbed the trees to get a better view.

A short diversion via the D115 from Daours leads to **Pont-Noyelles** where, on the hill, there is a monument of the 1870 Franco-Prussian battle. The views here are splendid.

The principal feature of the town of **Corbie** is the impressive bulk of the abbey church of St Pierre, a very early foundation of 657; what one now sees dates from the sixteenth-to-eighteenth centuries, though somewhat restored. It is apparently full of treasures but seems permanently locked. Across the square is a former Franciscan chapel, now a school, and to its north is a monumental eighteenth-century Doric gateway, looking more like the entry to the railway station than to an abbey. The Hôtel de Ville is brick-built in the picturesque Viollet-le-Duc Gothic Revival style – all round towers and pointed turrets. In front of it is the war memorial by Albert Roze, with a demure lady and child, and opposite, No 3 rue Victor Hugo sports Art Nouveau tiling. An old mill on the river is now occupied by a spectacular junk shop.

Across the river at **Fouilloy**, a suburb of Corbie, is a rather unusual 1958 church, the facade of which is decorated with thirteen flat sculptured figures in an anachronistic 1930s style, long after Matisse or Leger. These depict the life of St Martin, the patron saint of soldiers. The D23 now leads up the hill towards Villers-Bretonneux, where the German advance was halted, only 17 kilometres from Amiens.

The tower of Lutyens's Australian National War Memorial and Military Cemetery can be seen for many miles, dominating the valley of the Somme. The location of the cemetery is remarkable. Set back from the road, two sophisticated classical stone pavilions stand on either side of wide steps which lead up to an impeccably planted cemetery, set on the gentle 300 metre slope of the hill. Closing the view is a tall severe tower, rising above a wide screen wall with flanking pavilions, all beautifully detailed in white stone. The tower provides a viewing platform, the vertiginous access stairway of which projects externally at high level. The whole composition is a masterly and brilliant blend of architecture and landscape. The furled flags are cut in stone, a favourite motif of Lutyens which he also used at Etaples. It is impossible to be unmoved by the terrible list engraved on the walls of the names of so many dead soldiers. The monument was not inaugurated by King George VI until July 1938, little more than a year before the whole tragic business started all over again.

Return now to Corbie and take the D42 along the banks of the Somme. Continuing eastwards along the Somme, **Chipilly** provides an unusually sentimental sculpture of a soldier comforting a wounded horse. Commemorating the 58th London Division,

VILLERS–BRETONNEUX: Lutyens's Australian memorial

SERRE: The British cemetery

it was carved by Henri Gauquié – a rare instance of a French artist working on a British memorial. Some 250,000 work horses were killed in the fighting but their contribution seems otherwise uncommemorated. To the north of Chipilly, Baron Manfred von Richthofen, the Red Baron (so called because of the colour of his Fokker Triplane), crashed to his death on 21 April 1918. Surprisingly, there is nothing to mark the spot.

At **Proyart**, 8 kms to the south-east, is a bizarre French war memorial. A reduced *arc de triomphe* set in a somewhat unkempt small park, it is adorned with good bronze panels and some rather sentimental marble groups by Gourdon, representing the soldier's farewell in 1914 and his welcome home in 1918. Bronze trophies decorate the gate posts. Those in search of some light relief can either head north to **Bray-sur-Somme**, a pleasant little town with an old church, noted as a centre for angling or take a trip on the steam railway which runs between **Cappy** and **Dompierre**, also to the north

(the trip includes a visit to a small museum devoted to the military rail system). Cappy was the base for the Red Baron's Flying Circus.

17 kms due east is **Péronne**. Bombarded in 1870, battered in 1916 and in the path of Operation Alberich – the plan to carry out systematic destruction as the German army retreated – it is nevertheless not without interest. The Hôtel de Ville is an entertaining mixture of the Renaissance and eighteenth-century classic styles, and there are some characteristic 1930s school buildings. Enthusiasts of military architecture can explore the rather battered château, the remains of the extensive brick fortifications, and the Porte de Bretagne, the old town gate of 1602. Rivers and canals surround the town, but the port is not what it used to be. A huge museum of the Great War is planned to open in 1992, which will no doubt bring more visitors to a town not much used to general tourism.

There is a memorial to the 2nd Australian Division at **Mont St Quentin**, on the N17

MAILLY-MAILLET: *Sculpture on the church facade*

LA NEUVILLE: *Detail of the church facade*

CHIPILLY: *Gauquié's memorial*

FLERS: *Toft's memorial*

two kms north of the town, in which a gold prospector is standing against the horizon: the bronze figure is a post-war replacement of the 1920s original, destroyed by the Germans after 1940.

Continue on the N17 to the village of **Bouchavesnes-Bergen**, rebuilt after 1918 with Norwegian aid and the donation of an imposing statue of Marshal Foch by Firmin Michelet (hence the returned compliment of adding Bergen to the name of the village). Almost immediately to the north on the N17 is the French military cemetery and memorial chapel at **Rancourt**. Inside the chapel, the walls are crowded with memorial plaques; one commemorating a private soldier is democratically flanked by those of a duke and a viscount.

To the west is an area full of cemeteries – including a notable British one at **Combles**. To the south-west at **Mametz**, far out into the fields north of the village, is the 38th Welsh Division Memorial: an angry red dragon clutching barbed wire, inaugurated as recently as 1987. It was in Mametz Wood that the poet and rider to hounds, Siegfried Sassoon, having stormed the German trenches, nonchalantly sat down to read poetry.

Next is **Longueval**, and the South African National Memorial at **Bois Delville** or Delville Wood (known also as Devil Wood to the troops). Set among trees, this is a clever, theatrical composition by Sir Herbert Baker; the central triumphal arch is crowned with an equestrian sculpture by Alfred Turner, representing the twins, Castor and Pollux with a giant steed (a comment on the two races who had themselves so recently been at war). It was in the countryside to the east, towards Ginchy, that the rains liquified the earth into treacherous quicksands of mud which swallowed up those heavily-laden soldiers who slipped off the path in the dark. Their vertical corpses were often not discovered until decades later. Just to the north, above the so-called **Caterpillar Valley** (typical of the many names invented by British soldiers, and actually a tank route in 1916) is the New Zealand Memorial, also by

Baker: a simple obelisk set in a ring of trees and carefully placed on the skyline. It is best appreciated from a distance. Continue northwards along the D197 to **Flers**, the scene of the world's first tank attack. At the end of the village street is a memorial to the 41st Division, a striking figure of a soldier holding a rifle. Designed by Albert Toft, the figure is identical to that in High Holborn, London, outside Waterhouse's Prudential building. Nearby, at **Gueudecourt**, is the Newfoundland Memorial, a rather un-appealing bronze caribou, the emblem of Newfoundland, and a close relation to that at Beaumont-Hamel. In the hamlet of **Le Barque**, just to the north, Hitler was wounded by a grenade in 1916. Two British war cemeteries, early works by Lutyens, are nearby – at **Warlencourt** (where a new memorial is planned by the Western Front Association) – on the D929, and at **Grevillers**. Now close is the cheerless crossroads town of **Bapaume**, an evocative name in the literature of the First World War. It has been fought over very frequently since Roman times, and has little of visual interest. In the process of changing hands several times after 1914, and especially because the Germans mined and booby-trapped buildings when retreating in 1918, it was virtually flattened, and the 1920s rebuilding was not memorable. Its most notable features are the extensive cellars beneath the town, used as shelters since 1551 at least and open to visitors, and the excellent bronze statue by Louis-Noël (1891), of General Faidherbe striking a dashing pose. The nearby war memorial with a statuesque female below the inscription 'Pax', is by Lesieux and dated 1934.

From Bapaume take the D7 north west for 14 kms to **Ayette**, where the little Chinese and Indian Cemetery shows conventional War Graves Commission architecture politely orientalised. At **Adinfer**, 5 kms to the north-west, there is a 1914–18 War Memorial in which a serene lady can be seen incising the lettering. Pause on the way to admire the Art Deco lettering

on the Hôtel de Ville at **Achiet-le-Petit**.
From Ayette the D919 leads first to
Puisieux, where the brutalist Art Deco
church is definitely an economy model, and
then to **Serre**, where there are two British
cemeteries with powerful plain Doric
porticoes, and nearby a surprisingly good
French cemetery with 1930s period lettering
and a bronze panel by Léon Dauchin of a
poilu dying in no man's land.

Now take the D919 to **Mailly-Maillet**,
where the exterior of the church of St
Pierre is decorated with a wonderful
Flamboyant Gothic sculpture (1509),
illustrating the well-known episode from
Genesis of Adam and Eve banished from
paradise. This remarkable sculpture
apparently survived the First World War
thanks to the local *curé* who carefully
protected it with layers of sacking. The
church also has a 1920s sculpted south portal
– very much in the style of Duval and Gonse
– and, above, some mildly Art Deco stained
glass. Mailly-Maillet is a welcome oasis in a
landscape filled with tragic memorials. At
the south end of the village is a Baroque
memorial chapel of the Mailly family built in
1752 to an oval plan, but we must await
completion of its restoration to appreciate
its quality.

Now take the D73, and then the D163,
for several rather curious memorials,
somewhat at variance with the rest, such as
the figure of a kilted Highlander at
Beaumont, another Newfoundland caribou
at **Beaumont Hamel** and, nearby, the Ulster
Memorial, a replica of William Burr's
nineteenth-century Helen's Tower at
Clandeboye: it is very Celtic and rather
incongruous in northern France but, with its
melancholy screen of pines, fitting for its
purpose. The writer Hector Munro, known
as Saki, fell at Beaumont Hamel in 1916.
After the war Scott Fitzgerald came here
and his impressions were conveyed by his character Dick Driver in 'Tender is the Night'.

These curiosities are a rather inadequate
preparation for what is now to come, the
greatest monument in the north of France.

As you approach **Thiepval** along the D73,
the towering shape of Lutyens's finest
memorial can be seen from afar, riding the
horizon and brooding over the landscape of
the Somme. Thiepval – The Memorial to the
Missing – is perhaps, for the British, one of
the more familiar images of northern
France: a complex stepped pyramidal
structure, built of brick with stone detailing,
and pierced by a great arch with a series of
intersecting smaller arches. These elements
were echoed in his later design for Liverpool
Cathedral. It carries the names of the 73,357
soldiers missing after the Battle of the
Somme (including the writer 'Saki'), who
have no known grave. As with his Whitehall
Cenotaph, Lutyens created a masterpiece of
symbolic architecture; its sublime mass
poignantly conveys an eternal sense of
tragedy – on the first day of the Battle of
the Somme, 1 July 1916, nearly 60,000
officers and men fell, the most costly defeat
in the history of the British Army.

Not far from Thiepval, along the D929 at
Pozières, is the Memorial to the Missing and
Pozières British Cemetery, commemorating
the 14,690 men of the British 5th Army
who, again, have no known grave. The great
portico, with its flanking screens, designed
by W.H. Cowlishaw with sculptural details
by Laurence Turner, makes an interesting
comparison with Thiepval, a handsome
lodge, as it were, guarding the approach to a
grand mansion. George Butterworth, the
composer of songs from 'A Shropshire Lad',
who was awarded the Military Cross, was
killed in action here in 1916.

Nearby, in the village of **Bazentin**, at the
end of a grove adjoining the church, there is
a monument commemorating Lamarck, an
eighteenth-century naturalist whose theories
of the origins of man preceded Darwin's.
The base is curiously carved with prehistoric
beasts. At **Ovillers**, the church of St Vincent
has an unremarkable exterior but contains
good 1920s stained glass.

The Tanks Corps Memorial at Pozières,
an obelisk flanked by bronze models of four
different types of tank, marks the spot

THE SOMME: British cemetery near Albert

THIEPVAL: Lutyens's Memorial to the Missing

where the British tanks set off for their first battle in 1916. Now take the D929 towards Albert: at **La Boiselle**, by the junction with the D20, there is an excellent bronze low-relief panel of St George and the Dragon (sculptor not recorded), the Tyneside Irish and Scots Memorial. Nearby is the vast Lochnagar crater, the largest on the Western Front, caused by British sappers who had tunnelled beneath the German lines and detonated a mine on the opening day of the Battle of the Somme.

From afar, the tall towers of Notre Dame and the Hôtel de Ville make a fine sight, rising high above the roof-tops of **Albert**. Originally called Ancre after the nearby river, the town was renamed in 1617. During the First World War, Albert was largely destroyed by shelling during the battles of the Somme and the Ancre, and by the fighting that accompanied the German offensive of March 1918. The town's main claim to fame is the familiar story of the Leaning Virgin, still commemorated by postcards on sale in every *tabac*. (Albert is a town in which one can still buy pre-war postcards).

In January 1915 the gilded figure of the Virgin and Child that crowns the tower of the nineteenth-century Church of Notre Dame de Brebières was hit by a passing shell. Despite leaning out over the street at a most precipitous angle, it remained resolutely attached to the tower until April 1918, when the remains of the tower – which had been used by the Germans as an observation post, were destroyed by British shelling. Inevitably all sorts of legends became attached to the Virgin during her pendulous period, reinforced by Albert's traditional role as a centre of pilgrimage for the veneration of an eleventh-century carving of the Virgin.

After the war Albert was rebuilt, and the church was reconstructed to its original 1884 design, a *tour-de-force* of restoration by Louis Duthoit, the son of the original architect Edmond Duthoit – a favourite pupil of Viollet-le-Duc, whose father and uncle, coming from a long line of sculptors,

worked on the restoration of Amiens Cathedral. The gilded Virgin, by the Amiens sculptor, Albert Roze, is once more in place on top of the tower. It looks splendid at night, lit so as to appear to float in the sky. Architecturally the result seems curiously anachronistic – a sombre, apparently late nineteenth-century building actually dating from the late 1920s. But it is worth keeping a sharp look out for the contribution of the later period: dazzling Art Deco mosaics, excellent modern sculpture by Anne-Marie Roux, including an Entombment, and several distinguished portrait busts by Roze.

The Hôtel de Ville, free standing in the main square, is the other dominant building of Albert, neo-Flemish and conservative for 1931, but less heavy than the town halls of Flanders. The tall central tower rises above steep pitched roofs with picturesque dormers, and the brick facade is decorated by well sculpted relief panels, with the familiar themes of Peace, Love and Work. On the front steps is a memorial to the Machine Gun Corps. In the foyer is a very interesting panel, a resumé of local history, and then some art genuinely of the 1930s: stained glass on the staircase depicting the three main local industries, agriculture, machine-tool making and aircraft manufacture. Art Deco glass doors, bright as silver, lead into a reception room with murals by Moritz and stylish light fittings. Parts of the town have a genuine 1920s feeling, with a good variety of old shop fronts, cafés and period lettering, including early enamel Michelin signs. The Aux Trois Pigeons café near the church is well worth visiting as a period piece: its interior – and its ownership – have remained unchanged since 1929.

Not to be missed is the war memorial, a heavy structure of 1920s classicism featuring low-relief panels and, in the centre, an extremely depressed looking lady. A few yards to the west, a panel on the front of a house: 'A Ch'Boen St Berthlon' is a reminder that we are in Picardy, with its own language, which survives and indeed is

POZIÈRES: Tank Corps Memorial

ALBERT: **The Sower** *by the station*

LAMOTTE–WARFUSÉE: The church

being revived. The railway station should also be seen, with its huge glazed semi-circular entrance with flanking wings, and its surrounding buildings, including a massive grain silo featuring a panel of a sower of wheat, in a rather rough Flemish Art Deco. This group has more genuine architectural style than the rest of Albert's rather tame revivalism.

Amiens – Towards St Quentin

The N29 eastwards – the Amiens-Vermand Roman road, is dead straight and mostly uneventful, but boredom can be kept at bay by some exploration. Pause at the town of **Villers-Bretonneux** for its 1920s flavour, and for the picturesque ruins of a *fin de siècle* mansion, at one time the home of a local factory owner, and untouched since 1918. The town commemorates the valour of the Australians with streets named Victoria and Melbourne, stuffed kangaroos in the foyer of the Hôtel de Ville, and the Victoria School which was financed by the subscriptions of Australian children and contains a small museum. The Hôtel de Ville escaped the neo-Flemish tradition and achieved a neo-Georgian look, touched by Art Deco. The village hall looks like a pre-war aircraft hangar and the 1920s church of St Jean-Baptiste, with its tall and distinctive spire, is worth a glance for its stylish lamp standards which flank the front steps.

Some excitement is then supplied by a series of rather eccentric churches, regularly spaced between Amiens and St Quentin. Stop at **Lamotte-Warfusée**, where the exterior of the church of St Thomas is a strong blend of Art Deco and Viennese Art Nouveau styles, while inside are Arts and Crafts and Art Deco details, notably the stained glass and the stations of the cross.

An 8 km detour to the south along the D165 takes one to **Caix**, where the rather battered church, l'Exaltation-de-la-Ste-Croix, has Flamboyant Gothic details on the tower, and an eighteenth-century doorway. Nearby is a German war cemetery, sinister with black crosses. (French crosses are usually of white concrete whilst English graves are marked by white headstones.)

Rejoin the N29 to **Estrées**, where there is a real gem of 1959, the concrete A-frame church of St Quentin – a dynamic building with good stained glass, and excellent details such as the spiral staircase, the whole cheaply built and yet an object lesson in the stylish use of concrete in the Perret tradition. About 7 kms further on, when crossing the Canal de la Somme, you will see the rather extraordinary tower of the church of St Géry at **Brie**, a sort of engineering Art Deco, looking like the top of a radiator on a 1930s car. At the next village, **Mons-en-Chaussée**, the church of St Pierre has a squat rough stone tower decorated with a low relief panel of Christ on the Cross, flanked by angels, while at **Vermand**, 15 kms west of St Quentin, the church of Ste Marguerite has a pierced concrete spire, 1920s

ESTRÉES: 1950s church interior

technology in the Gothic style, sitting on a vaguely Romanesque building with 1925 stained glass from Nancy. The most astonishing thing, however, is the Romanesque font, carved from blue Tournai stone with wonderfully lively animals, birds and other creatures, presumably saved from the old church.

Amiens: South West Excursion

Take the N29 southwest from Amiens, and then turn eastwards on the D920. (If making a more leisurely tour, or if heading towards Normandy, take a wider sweep via the quieter D211 from Amiens. There are good views over the city from **Saveuse**, and a stylish 1960s white stone church at **Saisseval**, while **Hornoy** is a pleasant sleepy little town with attractive buildings, including a seventeenth-century market hall. On the outskirts, the neo-Classical château of 1780 in a lovely park, can be glimpsed from the road. Then turn eastwards via Poix-de-Picardie to the D920.)

The Selle Valley is attractive with its water meadows fringed by poplars, but the new road, on its northern slopes, has lost the intimate feel of the valley and bypasses all the villages. However, be sure to take the turning to **Frémontiers**, where there is a pretty mill, complete with its waterwheel while opposite is an eighteenth-century mill house, handsome and formal. Together they make a picturesque group. Nearby is the Flamboyant Gothic village church of St Pierre. Carry on to **Conty**, a pleasant town ranged around a typical square. The large church of St Antoine is Flamboyant Gothic with a nineteenth-century west front and an entertaining display of gargoyles reaching well out over the street – be sure to stay on the other side of the road if it rains.

From Conty take the D8 northwards, and you will soon come across two eighteenth-century châteaux. The first, **Tilloy**, is rather severe and dull, the other, **Wailly**, is much better. At one time an estate of some significance, Wailly consists of one wing of a large eighteenth-century house, which survived the Revolution, flanked by a curious rusticated hemi-cycle screen wall of 1781, and substantial outbuildings. It rises prominently out of the surrounding woodland. In the village above are a range of stone estate houses and cottages, and a church with a late Baroque facade, uncommon for village churches in Picardy. The house is private, but it can be viewed from the opposite side of the valley. Field-Marshal Montgomery stayed here on his way through France in 1944.

The road back to Amiens is along the agreeable D210, but there is a diversion for modernists to **Oresmaux**, to the east. A village of notable insignificance, but it includes the good 1957 stone built church of l'Assomption-de-la-Vierge which has a remarkably tall detached bell tower, a landmark for miles around, and sculpture by Despierre, reminiscent of Epstein. The interior has a large fresco and the stained glass looks good, if you can ever get in to see it.

Amiens: North Excursion

Take the N25 north to **Bertangles**, where there is a splendid Louis XV château, notable for the finely-carved trophies on its facade; it is easily viewed from the road through its enormous eighteenth-century wrought-iron gates by the master-forger Veyren, with sumptuous detail including lively hunting motifs. A bit further on is **Villers-Bocage**, where the church of St Georges has a sixteenth-century *mise au tombeau*, carved in a somewhat similar style to that at Doullens, but less refined. The Gothic sepulchre frames figures in Renaissance dress but the polychromy, though authentic-looking, is probably of the nineteenth century, since the painting of the striking sculpture of St George, near the high altar, was executed in a similar style at the turn of the century.

Turn left for **Naours**, where there is a vast network of man-made caves, twenty to thirty metres below ground, called *muches*. They provided refuge from barbarian

invasions in the third and fourth centuries, and, in the ninth century, from invasions by the Normans. In succeeding centuries, the local inhabitants were under frequent attack, and so developed what became virtually an underground town. At the time of the Thirty Years War, the Naours caves could house two thousand people, and the complex included underground chapels, stables, barns and even a bakery. They were used by English troops in the First World War and by Germans in the Second World War. It is now all part of what would nowadays be called a theme park, complete with reconstructed windmills.

Amiens: West Excursion

Take the Abbeville road, the N235, along the Somme's southern bank to **Ailly-sur-Somme** where there is the very distinctive post-war church of St Martin.

Signposts provide directions to Samara, on the north bank of the Somme. This important oppidum – a fortified site known as Caesar's Camp, is the focal point of a very serious archeological theme-park, beautifully situated on the banks of the Somme. In addition to actual prehistoric remains, there are reconstructed Celtic dwellings, demonstrations of early craft techniques, an aboretum and a botanical garden.

Now cross the Somme again to visit **Picquigny**. Built to defend one of the early crossing points of the Somme, the town is spread over the steep south side of the valley. The château, broken and battered, is a picturesque ruin, especially when viewed from the meadows to the south. Passing through the gateway, one is faced by the pleasing grouping of the castle walls and the church with its strong fifteenth-century tower. The upper terrace offers good views over the valley of the Somme. There is a Renaissance kitchen with an immense fireplace, and beside the main gate is a little Renaissance pavilion, inhabited for a time by Madame de Sévigné, and adorned with carved details of the period. However the most obvious feature of the facade, a bust, is patently recent. Nearby, an inscription in 1930s lettering records that Louis XI signed the Peace of Picquigny with Edward IV here in 1475 – thus ending the Hundred Years War.

Just across the river is the Abbaye du Gard, a Cistercian foundation of 1137 with a chequered history of destruction and rebuilding. In its heyday Richelieu was the abbot-superior. The abbey now consists of rather tame eighteenth-century buildings, recently restored by an order of monks who welcome paying guests seeking to go on retreat.

Having crossed the river by the D57, continue to **Flixecourt**, where the tone is set by a grandiose nineteenth-century château, of splendid bourgeois opulence. There are a number of rather grand villas and mansions, the fruits of the success of various local jute barons.

Just to the north, at **Vauchelles-les-Domart**, is a mellow Louis XIII château in a very formal classical style of brick with stone dressings, with a tall centre framed by long wings. Still in the hands of the de Lassus family for whom it was built, Vauchelles is now a hotel. 7 kms to the north, the pleasant small town of **Domart-en-Ponthieu** has a number of old buildings including a rather battered Gothic house with a war memorial by Roze standing in front. In the centre of the village of **Fransu**, 6 kms to the north-west, is a most appealing small eighteenth-century château easily viewed from the village street, set behind an ornamental ironwork clairvoyée.

To the south-west is **Long**. It is essential to approach it from the south, crossing the expanse of the river Somme. Above the water meadows is the exhilarating skyline of the village, formed by the vast nineteenth-century church with its spiky Gothic roof-line, the cupola on the Hôtel de Ville, and the mansard roof of the château, with its exquisite rose brick and white stone detailing. The church is actually rather dull, vital only as townscape, but the château is excellent, pure Louis XV, with carved panels, fine ironwork and a magnificent position. It is open to visitors in August and September. The most eccentric building is the Hôtel de Ville, a vast and pompous neo-Renaissance confection richly endowed with architectural fripperies, wholly disproportionate for what is only a village. Visually they are an exciting group, offering far more than the rather better known but tedious remains of the château in the Gothic Troubadour style set on an island in the river at **Pont-Remy**, 6 kms to the west.

Cross over the river to visit **Airaines** for its two churches. The chapel of Notre Dame has a very curious Romanesque font, and its priory buildings are now a cultural centre. The parish church of St Denis is sixteenth-century: its exterior is promising but access is not easy; it apparently contains good statues, a *mise au tombeau* and Renaissance stained glass. To the south, in the quaintly named village of **l'Arbre à Mouches**, is the plain château of **Tailly**, the home of General Leclerc: there is a statue of the hero on the driveway. His birthplace was the much better looking château of **Belloy St Léonard** in the remote wooded countryside 4 kms to the south-west, towards the Normandy borders.

A cross country route westwards for 20 kms leads to the château of **Rambures**, very close to the borders of Normandy. The powerful cluster of round brick towers with stone machicolations provide the modern visitor with a striking example of a feudal fortress dating from the period of the Hundred Years War. Rambures, which may be visited, has been in the hands of the same family since the fifteenth century. David de Rambures, who figures in Shakespeare's *Henry V*, was killed at Agincourt with three of his sons. To the north, there is the well restored windmill at **St Maxent**, while in the village of **Huppy**, the seventeenth-century château, which is sometimes open, was the headquarters of Colonel de Gaulle in 1940 (he was not made a general until later that year).

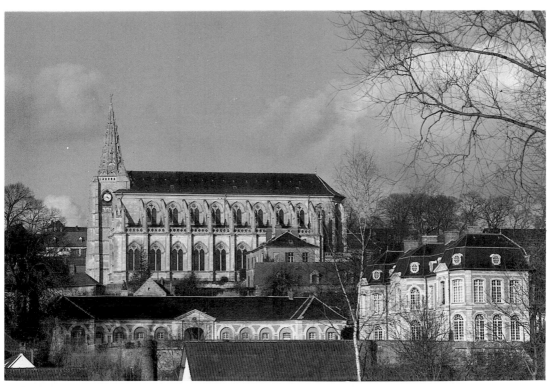

LONG: View of the church and the château

LONG: The château

RAMBURES: The château

41

ARRAS: The Beaux Arts Museum

ARRAS (Pas de Calais)

The Grand'Place at Arras, the old Corn Market, is a splendid experience. Of ancient origins, this enormous and complete cobbled square, some six hundred feet by three hundred feet, is formed by 155 tall Flemish Baroque gabled houses, mostly dating from the seventeenth and eighteenth centuries, all of grey stone and mellow brick, and built over arcades. The model for the architecture was the Gothic Hôtel des Trois Luppars (leopards) of 1460 at No 47, now converted into a hotel – but with no original interiors, alas. It was built when Arras, an important stage on the trade route from Provence to Flanders, held one of the principal fairs of the Middle Ages. Gothic was the model, but the Baroque triumphed, with an exuberance of swirling volutes, sirens, salamanders, unicorns and mermaids. The unity and harmony of the square is due to precepts of town-planning, but there are many delightful flourishes in the varied and often sumptuously carved stone details which give each house some individuality. Below the arcades are cellars, often several storeys deep. Although usually quiet and empty, the place is the setting for colourful medieval parades at Whitsun. Almost adjoining, and linked by a short street, is the Petite Place, or Place des Héros, a similar arcaded square, but more tightly enclosed. Filling the west side is the Hôtel de Ville, with its magnificent 80 metre belfry, built at such a proud height to remind us that Arras was among the first towns in France to gain the status of *commune* in 1194 – though it paid for its civic pride later, when Louis XI sacked the town in 1477 and deported many of its inhabitants. The belfry also served as a watch tower to warn the town of approaching invaders.

Despite its seemingly accurate and meticulous late-Gothic and Renaissance detailing, the whole structure is in fact a careful 1934 replica of the original, which was destroyed in the First World War and is the work of Pierre Paquet – better known to architectural pundits for his Pavillon de Haiti, in a sort of tropical-moderne style, for the 1937 Paris International Exhibition. Visits to the top of the belfry are highly recommended, providing excellent views over the town and the surrounding countryside – familiar to Corot who had a studio in Arras. Those without a head for heights might prefer to tour the cellars (known as *boves*), which were used as a shelter and a hospital for British troops. The interior of the Hôtel de Ville should be visited to appreciate its scale and grandeur. On the ground floor, in the Salle Robespierre, is a splendid Renaissance fireplace bearing the arms of Charles V and a bust of the revolutionary by Claudel. Upstairs, the vast and imposing Salle d'Honneur, is notable for its panelling carved by Seguin, its ceiling and its rather extraordinary frescoes, painted by Hoffbauer in the style of Breughel, a vast panorama fancifully depicting Arras life in the sixteenth century. In the Salle de Mariage is a powerful bronze bust of Marianne, who symbolises the might of the Republic, while the 1932 mural entitled 'Le Printemps' is by Gustave-Louis Jaulmes, a pupil of Puvis de Chavannes, best known for his murals for the 1925 Paris Exposition des Arts Décoratifs and has a suitably sylvan and romantic flavour. A mural in the Salle de Conseil, painted in the same year by Charles Hollart, but in a quite different artistic style, represents rebirth, work and peace. Ironically this room served as the Nazi Tribunal which deported thousands of locals. Downstairs in the foyer, the giants Colas and Jacqueline, representing actual personalities, stand patiently awaiting the next carnival. In the arcade facing the Place is a Resistance memorial, depicting a chained naked man, and more powerful than the usual weedy sculpture of the 1950s.

These two squares, which form a unique architectural ensemble, set the tone for this fine provincial town, the capital of Artois and the birthplace of Robespierre. Known originally for its textiles and tapestries –

those who know their Shakespeare will remember what happened to Polonius when he hid behind the arras – the town has enjoyed considerable wealth in its past, and this is reflected in its architecture. Much survives, despite extensive battering in both world wars. This destruction conceals the fact that the town was virtually rebuilt in the late eighteenth century, though largely retaining the old street pattern. Fortunately, many streets remain of these eighteenth-century houses, particularly near the Cathedral, their facades exhibiting an enjoyable variety of carved detail.

The former Benedictine abbey church of St Vaast (pronounced Va), dedicated to a sixth-century evangelist, and the cathedral since the Revolution, is a late eighteenth-century Classical stone structure, though to a Gothic plan, of very grand proportions, approached by a majestic flight of steps. The original design was by Pierre Contant d'Ivry, architect to the Princes Croÿ, de Conti and de Soubise, and the author of the first design for the church of the Madeleine in Paris. The vast interior, of luminous white limestone, is 102 metres long, 26 metres wide and 32 metres high. Giant corinthian columns are the dominant feature of the austere nave which is bathed in light. The tall statues in the aisles of saints, by Fremiet, Chapu and Hiolle were brought from Paris. When the church was restored after war damage, 1930s embellishments were introduced: stations of the cross, the bronzes of the main altar and the font by Saupiqué, the curious pulpit by Gaumont, and the immense reredos by Bouchard in the south transept, flanked by rather poor murals by Desvallières and Hollart. The mural painting of the cupola of the absidal chapel by Marret, depicting the life of the Virgin, is much more effective. All this modern church art fits in quite successfully.

In the small garden, by the north steps, is the 1930s bronze statue of a lady with a dove, by Maxime Real del Sarte, better known for his war memorials. To the north-west, the charming turreted 1635 Hospice St

Eloi stands in a leafy square, the place de l'Ancien Rivage, with the old quays of the river Scarpe nearby. Here on Bastille Day, 14 July, the locals dance the night away and enjoy a spectacular display of fireworks and music over the water. On other fête days, jousting on the water takes place. In the nearby rue du Crin, 1920s villas sport jazzy tile panels.

Returning towards the town centre, the rue des Teinturiers passes the west front of the cathedral and skirts the adjoining bishop's palace, the Palais St Vaast, a grandiose eighteenth-century building, designed by Labbé for Cardinal de Rohan, with wings nearly two hundred metres long enclosing spacious cloisters. At the end of the street, the characteristic 1930s Ecole Maternelle is placed with good effect on the corner of the rue Paul Doumer in which, on the left, will be found the gigantic gateway to the entrance courtyard of the bishop's palace, which now houses the Musée des Beaux Arts. The interior is suitably imposing. The galleried hall and spacious staircase have excellent wrought-iron work. The collection of paintings is extensive, from medieval to modern, but without any major excitements; however – quite apart from the scale of the architecture – given the variety of the pictures, the interesting room devoted to World War Two, with grim relics of the Deportation, and the large Tournai and Arras pottery collection – this is a museum which should not be missed. Look out for the fourteenth-century funeral mask of a young woman with an enigmatic smile, the gruesome 1446 black marble tomb of a decaying man covered in maggots, and the monumental eighteenth-century marble chimneypiece in the refectory, with its mantelshelf some eight feet above the floor. Close to the museum gateway, a plaque records that the Welsh Guards were the last allied troops to leave the town in 1940 (on 24 May), and the first to re-enter, in September 1944.

The nearby rue des Jongleurs, with a fine eighteenth-century town mansion, the Hôtel

ARRAS The Hôtel de Ville

ARRAS: The Grand'Place

ARRAS: The cathedral

ARRAS: The reredos in the cathedral by Bouchard

45

ARRAS: Place Victor Hugo

de Guines, leads to the place du Théâtre, which was the site of the guillotine – voraciously used in Arras, thanks to its particularly bloodthirsty mayor, Lebon. The neo-Classical theatre, of 1784 by Gillet, has its interior intact which is a rare treat, and it faces the jolly Baroque l'Ostel des Poissonniers, adorned with sirens and sea-gods. At No 7 bis is the headquarters of the Society of Orphéonistes or fanfare players. The nearby Salle des Spectacles – a play-house – has some lively thematic sculpture on its facade. The nearby rue Robespierre has sinister memories, including the home of the Revolutionary and the office of the detestable Nazi deportations of World War Two, which sent away 9,000 local people, not only Jews, to the death camps.

Just east of the Place des Héros, in the rue de la Housse, the charcuterie Jean Briet, with its nice old-fashioned marble and mosaic interior, has been here since 1879. The church of St Jean-Baptiste (a Temple of Reason during the Revolution) was rebuilt after 1914–18 war damage, but the Gothic tower survives, with its elegant octagonal

lantern. The interior should be visited for the stained glass designed by Hollart and d'Ingrand and the stations of the cross: sculpted half life-size by Jules Déchin, they vividly depict the drama of the crucifixion of Christ. A few steps on, the Chapellerie Modes is an excellent Art deco hat shop with stylish lettering. To the east, in the rue du Saumon, the Variétés, with its lively pink and cream facade, looks like an 1890s Music Hall but was actually built in 1924. The 1914–18 war memorial by F.A. Desruelles, in front of the station, has low relief panels of agricultural and military life, the themes of peace and war being expressed by a tractor and a tank. The bustling post-war station is of no visual interest but is destined to see a dramatic increase of bustle in 1993 when Arras will be served by the TGV high speed trains from Paris, 110 miles away; the journey will take a mere 50 minutes. The town is preparing for the future after 1993 by erecting on a site next to the station, a huge conference centre – the Centre d'Affaires Européen.

Back along the rue Gambetta, the main

street of the town, the mainly 1920s buildings have typical Art Deco flourishes of ironwork and mosaic. On the wall of the post office is a bronze portrait plaque of Joan of Arc by G. Proudhomme, of 1930, depicted here as a typical Thirties girl. She was imprisoned in Arras in 1430. The Hôtel du Commerce opposite is comfortable for an overnight stop. In the lobby, with its old-fashioned cage-lift, is an atmospheric painting of colonial days. To the south, in the rue Marguerite, a rather monstrous 1950s semi-circular school for girls is greatly improved by sculpture of females by Le Tourneur, in the style of late Leger or Maillol. The continuation of the rue Gambetta is the rue St Aubert. In a corset shop here, the Resistance heroine Berthe Fraser was due to meet the English agent Yeo-Thomas, code-named White Rabbit. After various upsets they managed to convey back to England the secret plans for V1 and V2 rockets. The rue St Aubert skirts a small square, the place du Wetz d'Amain, with a picturesque sixteenth-century gabled town house and a good statue of a prelate by Louis-Noël, and leads to a jolly and elaborate Neptune fountain, dated 1868, in the place du Pont de Cité. The church of St Nicholas-en-Cité, a few yards to the west, by local architect Joseph Traxler, is a dull neo-Classical building of 1838–46 which stands on the site of the old cathedral. The adjoining grand eighteenth-century building housing the préfecture, was formerly the bishop's palace. Around the corner in the rue d'Amiens are several early houses, notably No 65 with a large Baroque relief making a flourish. Southwards are a number of streets to explore with agreeable old houses and backwaters: the marché aux Poissons, a crescent of houses recently restored, the place du 33ème with an Art Deco fountain which deserves to be restored, the place de la Croix Rouge, the place St Etienne and the rue des Fours. The rue des Promenades contains workers' houses built in 1768 by a textile manufacturer, an early example of industrial

paternalism. Through the gateway of the 1920s Lycée in the rue des Quatres Crosses, with its good iron gates, a very distinguished eleven-bay eighteenth-century pedimented mansion can be seen (the Hôtel de Beauffort of 1754, though the sculpture is later), by no means provincial. Around the corner, No 30 rue des Capucins is a town house in the Art Nouveau style, which is uncommon in Artois.

The octagonal place Victor Hugo, with its obelisk, is an excellent setpiece of eighteenth-century town planning, often to be found in French provincial towns but uncommon in the North. This leads towards a major feature of the town, the Citadelle. Arras has been an important garrison town since the seventeenth century, the period of Louis XIV's territorial ambitions in the north, and its military architecture is on a suitably grand scale, with barracks, ware-houses and a riding school. Architecturally, the Citadelle (1670), in Vauban's char-acteristic style, is the major feature: a pentagon set within huge, brick, nine-pointed fortified ramparts, surrounded by moats, still partly filled with water. It is still firmly in military use and so it is not easy to pass through the splendid gateway to visit the Baroque chapel, but it is possible by arrangement with the Tourist Office. In the park opposite is a charming 1930s sculpted monument commemorating the 250th anniversary of the Rosati literary society. An eighteenth-century marquis and a modern man gaze upon a parade of muses. Further along the Boulevard Charles de Gaulle, an essential visit is to the Faubourg d'Amiens British Military Cemetery and Memorial to the Missing. Lutyens mastered the awkward siting, and created a long classical cloister which largely turns its back to the main road to enclose the Royal Flying Corps Memorial, a pylon upon which is a winged globe carved by Sir William Reid Dick.

A little track beside the cemetery leads past allotments to another memorial, the Mur des Fusillées. A quiet and secret place in the dry bed of the moat within the outer

MONCHY–LE–PREUX: 37th Division Memorial

VIS–EN–ARTOIS: Memorial to the Missing

fortifications, it movingly recalls the deaths of the 220 souls, many of them Polish miners and Communists, shot between 1941 and 1944 by the Hitleriens, as the bronze plaque puts it.

Arras: South & East Excursion

Immediately south of Arras there is not a great deal of interest. The former village of **Achicourt**, now almost a suburb of Arras, has an odd-looking 1920s church – St Vaast by Bonhomme and the Hôtel de Ville with the distinctive feature of the Croix-de-Guerre on its facade. But, to the south, one place which escaped the destruction of both wars in the region of Arras is the delightful spread-out village of **Rivière**, full of white limestone cottages and barns but with the distinction of a good eighteenth-century church dedicated to St Vaast, the pretty château de Grosville flanked by a tall *colombier*, and, on the southern edge, a picturesque creeper-clad *manoir*, its tree-shaped forecourt approached through a tall stone gateway with ornamental iron gates. Heading towards to the Somme battle fields, one cannot fail to notice the huge Beghin-Say sugar beet factory close to the D919, 11 kms south of Arras, a powerful example of modern industrial architecture.

The Cambrai road (the D939) should be taken eastwards for a few kilometres, first making a short detour north into **Monchy-le-Preux** for the memorial by Feodora, Countess Gleichen, to the 37th Division (her brother's Division) with its triumvirate of bronze soldiers (1920). In the village is yet another bronze caribou, a formidable beast, commemorating the fallen of Newfoundland. Continue then along the Cambrai road to **Vis-en-Artois** for the Memorial to the Missing of Artois and Picardy, a very successful design by J.R. Truelove. A great screen flanked by tall cenotaphs and Ionic colonnaded wings, in a particularly vivid white stone, it overlooks the graves of the cemetery, which are set out in curving ranks. The sculptural detail by Ernest Gillick is first-rate, notably the

VIMY RIDGE: View from the Canadian Memorial over Artois

VIMY RIDGE: The Canadian Memorial

VIMY RIDGE: The Canadian Memorial – a detail of the sculpture

crisply carved military trophies and a panel of George and the Dragon. In the village of Vis itself, the school and the Mairie form a pleasing 1930s group.

Return towards Arras and take the D37 to **Feuchy**. The small brick church of St Vaast is by Cordonnier, on a more modest and pleasing scale than his usual work, and inspired perhaps by the fortified churches of the Thiérache. The decorative brickwork, all in headers, frames a mosaic arch with a mandorla above, of the Virgin and Child. The stained glass within is by Jean Gaudin. In front of the Mairie is a war memorial by Déchin. The D37 then leads to the N50, and the large 9th Scottish Memorial sited between the dual carriage-ways. Rugged monolithic granite stones, inscribed with the names of battles, are arranged like a prehistoric monument, around a ruined tower. Going eastwards towards Douai along the N50, make a brief detour into the village of **Gavrelle**. The 1925 church of St Vaast by Marcel Bonhomme has stained glass of the period and, on the nearby green, an attractive war memorial looking like a classical wellhead, with a dedication to Ste Germaine. There are two war memorials in the village of **Oppy**, to the north – one was erected on land donated by Vicomte and Vicomtesse de Bouexic, in memory of their son and in addition commemorates soldiers from Kingston-on-Hull – the other, on the green in front of the 1931 church of St Nicholas by Bonhomme, is unsigned but in the style of Roze.

Arras: North Excursion

Take the N17 from Arras towards Lens. At **Roclincourt** there is a 1920s church and a curious war memorial, dated 1950, but clearly in a pre-war style. **Thélus**, a village now swamped by the motorway, has a simple stone memorial to the Canadian artillery. While not visually exciting, it is remarkable in that it was built by order of the Canadian General Byng in April 1918 before the end of the war, and long before most of the Great War monuments were built.

Take the well marked winding road up through the pine woods to **Vimy Ridge**, noting the shell craters and trenches, now overgrown, that still litter the landscape. There is no clue from the road of what lies ahead, so the impact is all the greater when a sudden clearing reveals the twin towers of the Vimy Memorial standing like sentinels on the horizon. The Canadian artist Walter Allward is not thought to be a great name among modern sculptors, yet anyone compiling a list of the most notable examples of twentieth-century monumental sculpture ought to include his Vimy memorial. For most of those who race south along the A26 auto-route, Vimy is just a fleeting glimpse of two towers crowning a distant ridge. It is all too easy to miss visiting this extraordinary structure, which commemorates not only the battle of Vimy Ridge of April 1917, but also the 66,500 Canadians who gave their lives during the First World War. Apart from its strong emotional quality, Vimy is remarkable because it has that perfect blend of sculpture, architecture and landscape that was once so common, but has become rare. The site itself is magnificent: from the crest of the ridge there are spectacular views for miles over the plains of Artois, dotted with the conical waste tips of coal mines. The strategic importance of the ridge is very apparent. At the car park there is a useful bronze map and a hut manned by young Canadians who distribute commemorative booklets; and then the long walk to the edge of the ridge and the memorial. Its huge scale and Allward's masterly use of the site soon become clear. Set into the steep northern scarp of the ridge, the design is complex, a mass of carefully balanced geometric and vertically thrusting forms which carry a series of large stone figures, the powerful symbolism of which is expressed in a style that combines the modernism of Rodin and Epstein with the sculptural traditions of the eighteenth century. The result is a dynamic Expressionist monument. Allward always claimed that the whole scheme came to him

MONT ST ELOI: View of the landscape

in a dream. Construction began in 1925 and was completed eleven years later. Only Lutyens's Thiepval memorial can compare with the grandeur of Allward's creation, but Vimy is perhaps made more exciting, and more moving, by its dramatic use of sculpture and its thrilling siting.

From Vimy take the D55 and D51, and you will quickly become aware of a structure ahead on a crest that is slightly reminiscent of the Sacré Coeur in Montmartre and, close by is a sort of lighthouse tower. This is **Notre Dame de Lorette**, the French national memorial and cemetery, commemorating primarily the ferocious battles of 1915 which took place here. There are 20,000 graves along the crest of the ridge, and the ossuary beneath the tower contains the remains of another 20,000 French soldiers whose identities are unknown. The scale of the cemetery is immense and what it represents is truly horrific, but the impact is lessened by the unoriginality of Cordonnier's architecture. The chapel is in a tired mix of

Byzantine and Romanesque styles, with an interior richly but unexcitingly decorated with marbles, mosaics and stained glass (some by the English artist Henry Payne). Equally dull in its detail, the tower is indeed a lighthouse, and at night its great lantern shines out for miles. Notre Dame de Lorette is simply not in the same league as the major British, Australian, Canadian or American memorials. Even the standard French military tombstone, seen here in such numbers, cannot compare with its excellent British counterpart. It is badly designed, with feeble lettering, and the use of concrete gives no sense of permanence. The best features of Lorette are the splendid views in all directions, particularly to the east towards the towers of Vimy. The contrast between the two could not be more marked. There is a small museum adjoining the cemetery on the east side. On the west side is a statue of General Maistre by Max Blondat. In the valley below, to the south, the ruins of the sixteenth-century church of

NOTRE DAME DE LORETTE: The French National Memorial and statue of General Maistre

NOTRE DAME DE LORETTE: French graves

Ablain-Saint-Nazaire are preserved as a memorial of the destruction of the Great War. A narrow lane descends to the D937 where a building housing the Artisanat d'Art Régional (a former diorama) has a frieze of 1914–18 battle scenes, by Robert Largesse.

At the main road village of **Souchez**, the Division Barbot memorial is a striking monument by Jules Déchin. Continue south on the D937 to the British **Cabaret Rouge** Memorial (named after a local café). Designed by Sir Frank Higginson, this has an unusual portal that blends strong classicism with Art Deco motifs. The ashes of Higginson, who died in 1958, are scattered here. Nearby, at **Neuville-St-Vaast**, are huge French and German cemeteries, along with smaller British ones. The artist Henri Gaudier Brzeska was killed here in 1915. Look out for a Polish memorial and a Czech cemetery facing each other across the main road, both with quite striking sculpture (the latter signed J. Hrvska 1925).

Neuville-St-Vaast was the birthplace of François Hennebique, the Tourcoing engineer who, from 1895, pioneered the use of reinforced concrete in the construction of buildings; his innovative designs paved the way for the striking and often daring use of concrete in France ever since.

Continue along the D937 and you will pass the rather bizarre French memorial by C. Yrondy at **La Targette** – a giant hand rising from the ground holding a flaming torch that looks suspiciously like a vast ice cream cornet. Now take the D49 towards the hill that carries the ruined eighteenth-century towers of **Mont St Eloi**, battered by the artillery bombardments of 1914. It is worth going up to Mont St Eloi for the view, and for a close inspection of the impressive remains of the abbey, originally founded in the seventh century. The artist E.H. Shepard painted the scene whilst on active war service, though he is better known for his drawings of Winnie the Pooh. In the summer of 1916, Ralph Vaughan Williams was stationed at Ecoivres in the little valley of the Scarpe just west of Mont St Eloi. He related in a letter to his wife Ursula that each evening he drove in the ambulance wagon towards Arras to collect the wounded, and described an occasion when "there was a wonderful Corot-like landscape in the sunset". One wonders if he was aware that Corot did indeed paint the local landscape. To the south on the D341, the water tower has been painted with very cheerful and decorative murals.

OLHAIN: *The château*

Leave Mont-St-Eloi on the D341 – it follows the ancient Roman highway from Lyon, now called the Chaussée Brunehaut, which continues, as Watling Street in England, all the way to Chester – go north-west for 11 kms, and then turn right to **Fresnicourt** to reach **Olhain**. Justifiably famous, and irresistably picturesque, the moated medieval fortress dates mainly from 1409, when it was rebuilt during the Hundred Years War. A gateway leads into an outer courtyard with ranges of pretty farm-buildings, still in active use. A draw-bridge then leads to the fortress; two massive towers and lower domestic wings are ranged around the inner courtyard, open at one end to overlook the moat to the countryside beyond. Olhain looks remarkably peaceful today, romantically reflected in the moat, with its swans and ducks. However the idyllic present conceals a turbulent past, since it was regularly besieged in the various wars which ravaged Artois. According to tradition, Olhain is haunted by a monk who killed a *seigneur* in the course of a drunken orgy. The château is open on Sunday afternoons in summer, but the buildings and their setting can be enjoyed from the drive, from which one can see both the view through the gatehouse into the central courtyard, and the château seeming to float gently in its moat.

As one continues northwards, the mining belt soon becomes evident. At the centre of **Bruay-en-Artois**, an active hub of the Resistance in the last war, is a particularly large and grim post-war school housing 2,700 pupils. However it is worth going into the impressive baronial Hôtel de Ville designed by René and Paul Hanote – only the clock gives away its date of 1931 – in order to see its highly effective stained glass windows by Alfred Labille depicting coalmining. Connoisseurs of social housing will be interested by the brown and yellow brick 1930s estates of miners' houses, planned on far more generous lines than their counterparts in South Wales. Jules Marmottan, the mayor and director of the local mines, enjoyed an alternative and more luxurious way of life in Paris. His mansion in the sixteenth arrondissement, containing his large collection of paintings and decorative arts, was bequeathed to the Institut de France by his son, and forms the basis of the famous Musée Marmottan. The nearby former mining town of **Calonne-Ricouart**, almost an extension of Bruay, has seemingly no attractions apart from the fine stained glass by Desjardins in the somewhat overblown Hôtel de Ville of 1930, designed in an expensive neo-Renaissance style by Albert

Godart. A short detour into remote country away from the mining belt, leads to **Bours**, 13 kms south west of Bruay. In the centre of the village, next to the interesting church of Ste Austreberthe, with its octagonal tower of 1586, stands a miniature fourteenth-century fortified château; toylike, it seems almost too small to be a serious fortress. A pretty route over undulating country may be taken via the D77 back towards the coast. The villages are marked by good churches, both ancient, at **Tangry** for example, and modern: notably the 1957 church of St Germain at **Fiefs** with a tall bell tower and a good low relief sculpture of the saint.

Marshal Pétain, the hero of Verdun and the unfortunate leader of the Vichy government, was born in a modest house on the Chaussée Brunehaut (D341) at **Cauchy-a-la-Tour**, 7 kms north-west of Bruay.

If continuing on this road towards the Channel ports, 12 kms north-west of Cauchy is **Estrée-Blanche** where the picturesquely turreted late medieval château of Creminil stands surrounded by moats. In the adjoining village of **Liettres**, the fortress, with walls four metres thick, powerfully evokes the feudal past of Artois.

Arras: South-west Excursion

On the outskirts of the town, the road towards St Pol (N39) passes the 1966 church of St Paul, with its striking silhouette. Turn left on the D339 for the valley of the river Gy, heading towards Frévent, a lush pastoral area of sleek cows grazing in water meadows. The villages have much charm and this route should be taken at an enjoyable amble, turning off to the left or right as you wish. The late Gothic church of St Nicolas in the pleasant little town of **Avesnes-le-Comte** deserves a look, and a detour should be taken to **Barly**, 4 kms to the south, to see the vivid white limestone château, built c.1782 in a rather feminine neo-Classic style, standing in the centre of the village opposite the church of St Léger, whose pediment echoes that of the château. An avenue of trees leads to a spacious courtyard attractively enclosed by an ensemble of outbuildings and a private chapel. The enthusiastic chatelain since 1970, the comte d'Antin de Vaillac, who saved Barly from ruin, guides the visitor (by appointment: Tel 21 48 41 20) around the surprisingly small and intimate rooms: the entrance hall with charming reliefs of the Four Seasons, the tiny panelled salon, the dining room with good plasterwork and the staircase hall with an elegantly curving carved and gilded wooden staircase, in a style which is a particular feature of this part of Artois. Another agreeable visit in the locality is to the late eighteenth-century château of **Grand-Rullecourt**, 6 kms due west, in course of restoration by the new owners, the Vicomte and Vicomtesse de Saulieu with their five children. Patrice de Saulieu O'Toole edits the Relais Routiers Guide founded by his father; his wife, née Chantal de Chabot Tramecourt is a member of the family who fought at Agincourt. They have some way to go with the restoration, and to raise funds, concerts are held and *chambres-d'hotes* are ready for paying guests. (Tel. 21 58 06 37). But the major sight is at **Frévent** – the château of Cercamp, a onetime Cistercian abbey and now a grand 1710 mansion, approached via an avenue of trees and a handsome gatehouse with curving wings. Foch established his headquarters here in 1915. Cercamp is the work of Raoul Coigniart, the architect of Valloires, and both these buildings contain panelling by Pfaff de Pfaffenhoffen, the Viennese sculptor.

LE GRAND-RULLECOURT: The château

AVESNES-SUR-HELPE (Nord)

Set on a hill above the river Helpe, Avesnes has an old-fashioned air that verges on the decrepit in the narrow streets that lead up to the main square. The square itself is enclosed by handsome eighteenth and nineteenth-century buildings, some old shop fronts and, in the centre, a powerful eighteenth-century Hôtel de Ville in the local blend of red brick with the blue stone of the region; it is approached by elegantly curving steps. At the far end of the square is the brick church of St Nicolas of 1534, with a strong stone tower; nearby, the presbytery is a surprisingly English-looking eighteenth-century house, with a pleasingly overgrown garden offering fine views from the remains of the Vauban fortifications. According to a plaque on the gate, Napoleon lodged here before giving the last orders of the day, on the eve of the Battle of Waterloo, and in 1870 the Imperial Prince stayed here before fleeing the country. Near the station is a sculpture commemorating a revolutionary drummer boy, inscribed '1793, A Moi les Patriotes', modelled by Léon Fagel in 1905. Jesse de Forest, one of the founders of New York, was born in the town in 1575.

Avesnes: West Excursion

Only those seriously interested in architecture will take the N2 southwards for 16 kms to **La Capelle** to see the church, and wonder how an architect of the calibre of Garnier, designer of the Paris Opéra, could produce such an indifferent building. There is also a racecourse, but more interesting is the armistice monument at **Pierre d'Haudroy**, 3 kms east along the D285. On 7 November 1918 emissaries from the German High Command came to La Capelle to discuss terms for the Armistice, and four days later the ceasefire was sounded here. The villages to the west of La Capelle, in the Nouvion forest, are famous for the making of sabots or clogs.

West of Avesnes, the D962 leads to **Maroilles**, a village famous for its strongly-flavoured cheese, which can be bought in local shops, and which is celebrated at an annual festival. It is a remarkably pretty place, still largely eighteenth-century, visually interesting because of the way in which the main street twists and turns, creating a series of pleasing triangular spaces. There is a good simple eighteenth-century church in the centre, dedicated to St Humbert, with unusual memorial plaques on the outside and, at the north end, a large and rather English tree-lined village green, with a big bandstand in the centre. Set in one corner is an 1807 triumphal arch. 5 kms to the west is **Landrecies**, with a central square dominated by a strong, though blandly detailed, Hôtel de Ville built in 1807, but restored. In front is a statue by Léon Fagel, of the local hero Dupleix, who established French power in India; it has suitably oriental details. His birthplace is nearby. Across the square is the pretty Art Nouveau facade of a former Au Printemps store. West of the town is the river Helpe, and on the bridge is a plaque commemorating General Sir Ronald Charles, who liberated the town from the Germans in November 1918.

To the north of Landrecies is the great oak forest of **Mormal**, covering over 900 hectares. Within the forest are **Locquignol** and **Hachette**, where there is one of a chain of pumping stations built to supply water to a canal cut to link the rivers Oise and Sambre. In operation by 1859, the pump was powered by a vast steam engine, which remained in continuous use until 1974; now redundant, but still in working order, the works can be visited. Beyond is Belgium and the fringes of the Ardennes. The villages and towns, traditional in feeling, with many eighteenth-century buildings in the local blue stone and red brick, are conventionally attractive, but rarely exciting.

Avesnes: East Excursions

Riverside mills, and factories, many now disused, reveal the former importance of the textile and other trades. At **Fourmies**,

AVESNES-SUR-HELPE: The church tower and roofscape

BAILLEUL: The interior of St Vaast

16 kms south-east by the D42, a textile mill built in 1874 has become an *éco-musée* – French shorthand for a museum of ecological interest). At **Sars-Poteries**, 9 kms north-east by the N2 and the D962, there is a glass museum, also an ancient watermill where traditional pottery is still produced. One of the best villages is **Liessies**, 14 kms due east by the D133, and attractively situated on the river Helpe. The church of St Lambert and Ste Hiltrude has rural Baroque details, and a twelfth-century Byzantine cross inside. An enjoyable small town is **Solre-le-Château**, 5 kms east of Sars-Poteries, handsomely built around an attractive square dominated by a sixteenth century Hôtel de Ville of pink brick, with restrained Renaissance decoration. Close behind, and seemingly growing out of its roof, is the powerful 1610 tower of the church of St Pierre, all in the local blue stone. The village church of St Martin at **Lez-Fontaine**, 2 kms west of Solre, has remarkable ceiling paintings of 1531.

BAILLEUL (Nord)

This was the original home of the Balliol family (de Bailleul) which provided two kings of Scotland, and founded Balliol College, Oxford. At first sight it seems a prosperous, well-preserved place, full of old Flemish houses, its central square dominated by a typical Hôtel de Ville with a massive belfry. A more careful look reveals a rather different story. Bailleul was a front line town for most of the Great War and was virtually flattened by the British. What stands today is a fanciful and romantic Flemish recreation, inspired by paintings of the Golden Age by such artists as Cuypers. It is not all that easy to discern the genuine pre-1918 houses from the 1920s replacements, but the occasional bullet hole or shell damage gives a useful clue. Although extraordinarily anachronistic, the overall effect is attractive, if a little dour, thanks to the use of the rather dark red brick characteristic of Flanders. In creating this revival of a traditional Flemish style, the builders were inevitably influenced by the trends of the 1920s – which is just as it should be, so avoiding direct pastiche. The result is a decent and harmonious architecture with extensive use of decorative brickwork and wrought-iron work. The hanging street signs are a good example of the latter. The proud Hôtel de Ville is actually of 1932, a successful design by Louis Cordonnier. On the outskirts of the town, on the D23, the hospital, famous in the First World War, has a good Art Deco gateway, and there are two largely early 1930s churches within the town. The more modern is St Amand, with its powerful tower: its light interior features a remarkable roof of exposed concrete, simulating timber beams, decorative brickwork of high quality, and mosaic work on the altar, pulpit and confessional. However, the main church is St Vaast, behind the Hôtel de Ville. It is more conventional, in an anachronistic Arts and Crafts style, with good mosaics, light fittings and painted decoration inside, but it looks as though it should have been built in 1892 rather than 1932. The belfry in the Hôtel de Ville can be visited by those seeking a view over the Flemish plains, and there is a small local museum nearby, the Musée Benoit de Puydt, where the charmingly eclectic collection of paintings, Persian rugs, furniture and ceramics are well-displayed in a house that once belonged to a former clerk of the court.

Nearby is a school of lace-makers, endowed by an American with the improbable name of William Nelson Cromwell, in memory of his wartime service here. The school sustains a long tradition in Bailleul of lace-making, and is housed in a vaguely Arts and Crafts style building.

The curious war memorial – a dramatic bronze angel with flying drapery in the style of Rude – whose best-known sculpture is the 'Marseillaise' on the Arc de Triomphe in Paris – is attached to the ruins of a church which was destroyed in 1918. Near this is a good eighteenth-century stone building, once the palace of justice but now a school, a surprising survivor. The impact of the war can also be measured by the large military cemetery, with over 4,000 graves of British, French, Germans, Russians and Chinese, as well as other nationalities. A favourite game of the locals is *boule flamande*, a rather hazardous version of the conventional French sport, which uses wooden discs weighted with clay instead of the more familiar heavy steel balls.

Bailleul: Excursion

Approaching Bailleul from the south along the A25 motorway from Lille – from which are splendid views of the towers rising above the town – pause in the layby 4 kms before the Bailleul turn-off, to admire an extraordinary farm close to the motorway near **Nieppe**. It has been decorated with all manner of aeroplanes, rockets, guns, helicopters and other fantastic machines, all made from scrap – French eccentricity at its best. It is actually within the commune of **Steenwerck** and in this village itself, the 1920s church of St Jean-Baptiste has a very striking tragic figure of Christ on the Cross, placed over the entrance portal; on the green opposite, the heroic figures of soldiers on the war memorial, are by the Rouen sculptor, Richard Dufour. In the street flanking the church is another of those houses with 1960s naive decoration; the whole facade of which is adorned with a tree in leaf, carried out in painted plaster.

Along the D933, 3 kms to the west of Bailleul, at **Méteren**, the 1920s church of St Pierre-et-St Paul is of quite an original design, with its tympanum decorated with ceramics. Inside are good stained glass, and stations of the cross featuring low-relief ceramic sculpture and mosaics.

Now take the D318 and D10 into pretty hilly countryside, to the village of **Berten**. The 1964 church of St Blaise was designed by Thibault; his good economical design

NIEPPE: *Home-made sculpture*

built in brick allowed the budget to include some charming stained glass depicting the Life of Mary, with other windows which double as stations of the cross.

Opposite the church a road climbs up to the hill village of **Mont-des-Cats**, crowned by the Trappist monastery, whose monks produce a well known cheese of the same name. The writer Marguerite Yourcenar, the first female member of the Academy (her nom de plume is an anagram of her maiden name de Crayencourt) was brought up here. Her autobiographical work, 'Archives du Nord', evokes the spirit of Flanders. A small museum in homage to her has been opened at **St Jans Cappel** (May to October, Sundays only 3–5).

In this undulating part of Flanders close to the Belgian border, where Flemish is the local language, are a number of windmills and the traditional inns called *estaminets*. At **Boeschèpe** a restored windmill, called l'Odankmeulen, or le moulin de l'Ingratitude, stands on top of a hill, beside an equally restored, but still remarkably original *estaminet*, complete with old-fashioned bars heated by tiled stoves and with a rumbustuous atmosphere. Nearby, at **Godewaersvelde**, there is an even better example, original and unrestored, with cheerful brightly-painted shutters. At **Eecke**, a village with a number of old houses, is the *hallekerke* church of St Wulmar, with a rare example of a detached timber belfry, called locally a *klockhuis*.

For enthusiasts of windmills, there are two at **Steenvoorde**, a few kilometres to the west – tall, well-restored wooden post mills dominating the approach to the village. Equally powerful is the modern pierced spire on top of the old church tower, a central focus for streets which are pleasantly lined with brick houses of all periods. Steenvoorde is also a good place for those who appreciate giants, with three members of the species, Jean le Bucheron, La Belle Helène and Gambrinus, on cavalcade in October at the annual Festival of Hops.

Excursion east of Bailleul

About 12 kms east of Bailleul is **Armentières**, a name made familiar by the popular song of the First World War about a young lady of the town. A more lasting impression has been made by the town's breweries and textile factories – a beer museum is housed in one of them – but the impact of the war cannot be overlooked. Armentières was, from October 1914 to

58

GODEWAERSVELDE: An estaminet

BOESCHÈPE: The windmill and estaminet

BOESCHÈPE: Interior of the estaminet

August 1917, the southern pivot of the British lines, and never more than a couple of miles from the front. The town was virtually razed during the German advance of 1918, including the old quarter and the original belfry.

Today there is a busy main square overlooked by the big 1920s Hôtel de Ville, a characteristic design by Louis Cordonnier. Inside, above the staircase, stained-glass panels by Morin depict the two principal local industries, textiles (now much depleted) and brewing, and there are scenes of the town by a local artist, Baude. Nearby, the church of St Vaast is also by Cordonnier. The brickwork is highly decorative, and the nave a fine space with mosaic and encaustic tile decoration, but it is not a really memorable building. It is flanked by the former market building, again by Cordonnier, now flashily converted to other uses. The War Memorial nearby, by Edgar Boutry, has animated low-relief panels on the base. It is decidedly better than the dull Resistance Memorial on the Nieppe bridge outside the town, which for reasons best known to itself, Michelin picks out as one of the most imposing in the North.

In the rue Jean Jaurès, in the courtyard of the former premises of the Frères Mahieu, textile factory owners, is a good bronze statue of the brothers as war heroes – they were both killed in action. The D945 leads westwards out of the town and passes the Lycée Technique, a big building by Chipiez of 1883 with lively decorative brick detail. Soon after, a turning to the right leads to the Cité Bonjean British Military Cemetery with its typical, elegant entrance loggia of pink brick in the Lutyens tradition. The road continues to a huge brewery, the Brasserie Motte-Cordonnier – a late nineteenth-century industrial building thankfully still in active use. Beer production remains an important industry of the North. Its traditions stretch back to at least the fourteenth century when Flemish weavers crossed the Channel and introduced hops to Kent.

BETHUNE (Pas de Calais)

A bustling town in mining country and a major canal port, Béthune was once fortified by Vauban; but not a great deal of any age remains to be seen, thanks to the German offensive of April 1918, so one can largely devote one's attention to the Grand'Place, a handsome square with a range of tall, narrow, houses topped with eccentric Flemish gables heavy with masks, cannons, foliage and other motifs carved in stone, in a blend of traditional and Art Deco styles: some are by Jacques Alleman, and were built in 1923. These houses look onto the fourteenth-century belfry tower, which now stands detached in the middle of the square, facing the large 1928 Hôtel de Ville, the interior of which is reminiscent of Odeon cinemas and was obviously influenced by the 1925 Paris Exposition des Arts Décoratifs – from which the term Art Deco derives. In view is the huge church of St Vaast, rebuilt by Cordonnier after the Great War, which makes a strong statement in the townscape and is characteristic of his work, imposing but unexciting, in this instance in the Gothic style. The sculpture of the entrance portals is worth a glance, enlivened with masks: evil grimacing at goodness. The interior has much bright mosaic detail and the sculpture includes a St George by Real del Sarte, a bishop by Déchin, the inevitable Joan of Arc and a copy of Michelangelo's Resurrection. More poignant for the British visitor is the memorial to one million dead of the British Empire "who mostly remain in France". Two minutes walk away to the north, in the rue du Tribunal, will be found the Musée de Béthune, houses in a fine 1750s mansion, the Hôtel de Beaulaincourt, its sturdy facade onto a forecourt lightened by gay Rococo motifs. The interior, in course of renovation, has panelling and painted overdoors of the period and contains a pleasantly eclectic collection – views of the town, weird paintings by Augustin Lesage (1876–1954), a *fin de siècle* barber's shop and an old café interior. The museum stands on the corner of the rue Sidi Carnot – at the northern end of this street, 200 metres away, enthusiasts of 1930s stripped classical buildings, will appreciate the Palais de Justice, in the so-called Fascist style. On the southern outskirts of the town, a supermarket has been installed in an enormous and impressive circular former railway building, another example of imaginative reuse of defunct industrial buildings in the Lille region.

One foot-note concerning the aftermath of the Great War: the City of Bristol, as a gift to the town, commissioned the architect W.H. Watkins to design cottages and flats to be built in Béthune.

Béthune: North East Excursion

Some curiosities are to be found north-east of Béthune, along the D171. At **Le Touret**, near J.R. Truelove's rather unsatisfactory cloistered memorial to those who died in the battles of 1914–15, there is one of those extraordinary primitive follies the French do so well – a little house covered with naive sculpture and ornaments, with a dominating statue of Marshal Foch on a horse perched on the front of the house with, above it, a structure looking like an early airport control tower. It commemorates the hero of its builder, Monsieur Wallart, who died in 1960.

At **La Couture**, 2 kms further north, is the powerful but decidedly eccentric Portuguese war memorial – a bronze soldier desperately keeping the grim reaper at bay with his rifle butt, with above him a tough-looking woman, whose loyalties are unclear. It is attached to a section of ruined church wall, in the style of the memorial at Bailleul; the sculptor was Teix Lopez.

Continue now cross-country eastwards for about 5 kms to **Neuve-Chapelle**, where there are two unusual memorial cemeteries. The Portuguese link is maintained by their Portuguese military cemetery, approached by a large and crudely detailed arch in a vaguely Manueline style – the elaborate Portuguese version of sixteenth-century Gothic. Much

BÉTHUNE: The Grand'Place, Belfry and St Vaast

LA COUTURE: The Portuguese war memorial

NEUVE-CHAPELLE: *The Portuguese military cemetery*

NEUVE-CHAPELLE: *The India Corps Memorial*

more appealing is the nearby cemetery commemorating the India Corps – the Indian Memorial to the Missing. Designed by Sir Herbert Baker, and one of his most attractive works, the stone structure is circular in plan and on quite a small scale, in a charming mixture of classicism with Indian motifs. A gateway leads into an intimate garden with a loggia, enclosed by pierced stone walls. The curious sculpture is by Sir Charles Wheeler.

Those interested in the works of Cordonnier can now proceed northwards to **Fleurbaix**, where there is one of his churches, albeit a dull example.

Béthune: South East Excursion

Leaving Béthune by the Lens road, the N43, you will pass the Dud Corner Memorial to the Missing, at **Loos-en-Gohelle**. A fairly conventional design by Baker, it contains the names of over 20,000 soldiers, including Rudyard Kipling's son, who died in the various conflicts, and in particular in the Battle of Loos – where the British used poison gas for the first time, in September 1915.

Lens, a mining town since 1841, was gravely damaged in the 1914–18 War, when its population was reduced by half. Some 150,000 miners came from Poland after the war to fill the gap. It lies in the heart of the mining area of Artois called la Gohelle, dramatically described by Emile Zola in his disturbing novel *Germinal*, and has been regularly fought over since the fifteenth century.

Although quite a lively place, there is little of visual interest but it is just the sort of town that one might expect to produce the champion boxer Georges Carpentier and Maurice Garin, winner of the first Tour de France in 1903. Racing-pigeons and cock-fighting are two of the local preoccupations. The main streets radiate from a central square of no great style, dominated by a vaguely classical church. However, perseverance will bring its reward, notably a rather crudely-carved but dynamic War

LENS: *The station (1928)*

CARVIN: *The church of St Martin*

LENS: *The station mosaics*

Memorial in the avenue Alfred Van Pelt, sculpted by Lesieux and designed by Barthelet, featuring lumpy ladies, noble workers, sturdy soldiers and the odd bomb; but the best feature of the town is the splendid 1928 railway station, by Urbain Cassan, who also designed Brest station in Brittany, graced with a modernist clock-tower in pierced concrete, and social-realist mosaics by Labouret, of miners, pits, steam trains and so on in the booking hall.

A skyline of pit winding gear, is still present but the machinery is quietly decaying. The miners' houses, called *corons*, are gradually being replaced and the huge Bureau des Mines, by Cordonnier, is now given over to university use. The memory of the 1200 miners who died in a single pit disaster early this century, is slowly fading. The miners' hero, Emile Basly, a Lenin look-alike, is commemorated by a statue in the avenue A. Maes.

The area around Lens is flat, a conurbation stretching as far as Douai – a grey landscape with patches of green, pierced by busy commercial canals and dominated by the huge cooling towers of **Courrières**. This one-time village was the home of the artist brothers, Jules (the Academician, and thereby a powerful figure of the art Establishment) and Emile Breton, the latter commemorated by a statue opposite the sixteenth-century church of St Piat which managed to survive the Nazi destruction in 1940. Van Gogh paid them a visit in 1879 but did not linger and nor will the tourist.

10 kms north-east of Lens is **Carvin** with a relic of its pre-industrial past: the church of St Martin, commissioned by Prince d'Epinoy in 1702. The splendid tower is in a particularly sturdy provincial Baroque style which is uncommon in the North. Its silhouette (although not its fussy detail) would look quite at home in an English country town. The unsigned 1914–18 War Memorial is well executed.

10 kms due east of Lens is the town of **Hénin-Beaumont**, until recently called Hénin-Liétard. The Hôtel de Ville, in a Renaissance style, is handsome enough but the reason for coming to this otherwise rather dim town is the church of St Martin, its monumental dome looming high above closely crowded roof-tops. The architect, Boutterin, was clearly inspired by Byzantine models but the result, executed in concrete in 1932, is quite eccentric. The dramatic interior is more successful than the exterior, with a profusion of good craftsmanship – metal-work, mosaic, stained glass by Jean Gaudin, and mural decoration. The stations of the cross are especially remarkable, Christ depicted in agonising close-up.

Head now south-westwards to **Rouvroy**, passing through **Billy-Montigny**, which seems to have only one feature of interest: the facade of the Art Deco Salle d'Oeuvres Sociales – a theatre for the community devoted to serious socialist works. The locals seem now to have abandoned edifying theatricals in favour of pop concerts.

At Rouvroy, the most obvious church is the conventional St Géry and it is necesssary to ask for directions to St Louis, which is a quite different kettle of fish – an early and highly original work by Duval & Gonse (see the entry for Roye). Below a tall, slim, plain brick tower, a porch with a sculpted panel depicting St Louis, leads into an immense octagonal space with the low arches of the transepts supported by short stubby columns. The detailing is generally simple and austere, the space lit by plain coloured glass. Until recently, the principal decoration consisted of mural paintings by H. Marret; these have been scandalously painted over by the Polish community who now occupy the church. Only the north doorway hints at the Art Deco period. The surrounding miners' houses are preserved by the parish, in opposition to the local mayor who is busily building smart new social housing – overlooked however by that ever present reminder of mining in Artois – the coal tips, their slopes albeit softened by green scrub.

Due west of Lens is **Liévin**, whose 1926 Hôtel de Ville by Jean Goniaux, is built of white limestone in an expensive Renaissance style with inside, on the stairs, a stained glass window by Alfred Labille depicting miners leaving the pit-head. At **Aix-Noulette**, 6 kms to the west, the church of St Germain dates from 1552 but was restored by Paquet after war damage. The main interest now is the contribution of post-1927: the statues of saints by Georges Laurent, Saupiqué and Alexandre Descatoire, the stations of the cross in bronze by Henri Bouchard and the stained glass designed by Magne and executed by Léglise, both of Paris.

The D937 now leads to Béthune via **Nœux-les-Mines**, which has a water-tower looking like a giant 1950s vase, a 1930s cinema with Art Deco details including stained glass, now a giant junk shop, and a 1950s house with jolly mosaics.

BOULOGNE-SUR-MER
(Pas de Calais)

So called to distinguish it from Boulogne-sur-Seine near Paris. But it is to this Boulogne that such conquerors as Claudius, Charlemagne, Napoleon, and Hitler came to contemplate our island and it was from here that Julius Caesar launched the invasion of England in 54 BC. In 1801 the port was unsuccessfully attacked by Nelson, with many British casualties.

Boulogne is the premier fishing port in Europe; as a port it was an inevitable target for bombing in the Second World War. Approached from the sea you can enjoy a good view of the town and its setting: high up, against the skyline, the dome of Notre Dame dominates the *Ville Haute*, framed by low hills. Below, modern tower blocks march along the waterfront, silhouetting the gaunt black hulks of the steel works in the foreground. To the left of the port is the town's playground: the sandy beach, the nearby Casino and the huge new marine museum which is under construction.

The bustling *Ville Basse* (lower town), which adjoins the port, had a large English colony in the nineteenth century –

numbering some 7,000 by 1857 – with their own clubs, churches and newspapers. Their activities were described by Thackeray and Dickens, who enjoyed several summer holidays here, and were much teased in Punch magazine. The explorer Sir Richard Burton met his wife in Boulogne and the American author, Henry James, who spent unhappy days as a child in one of the many local English schools, later featured the town in one of his novels, *What Maisie Knew*. In the nineteenth century the town was the world centre for the manufacture of steel pens. Gillot's experience here enabled him to set up in Birmingham. The great event for the colony was the visit by Queen Victoria and Prince Albert in 1855, when they arrived in the royal yacht en route for Paris, at the invitation of the Emperor.

The *Ville Basse* has been mostly rebuilt along the water front, the protecting estuary of the river Liane, in a predictable mass-produced post-war style. But in the rue Pot d'Etain, an eighteenth-century house survives, now a restaurant; it was the birthplace of the writer and critic Sainte-Beuve, and is marked by a portrait plaque by Vernier. Adjoining the port is a good sandy beach, the subject in its heyday of a painting by Manet. Next to the Casino is a monument to the famous Comédie-Française actor brothers Coquelin, and an enormous new museum in course of construction – the Centre Nationale de la Mer.

Just to the east, adjoining the bridge, le pont Marguet, the tourist office is housed in a small octagonal Art Deco pavilion which faces a monument (by J. Lafrance 1880) to Frédéric Sauvage (died 1867), who pioneered the use of the helical screw to propel ships.

The Grande Rue climbs gently away from the port. Something of the old atmosphere of the *Ville Basse* becomes apparent in the attractive cobbled market-place, presided over by the largely eighteenth-century church of St Nicolas (by Giraud Sannier, 1774), its bold facade with giant volutes looking rather like a stage setting for an opera.

BOULOGNE-SUR-MER: The basilica and walls of the Ville Haute

To the west, in the rue Thiers, is the famous Philippe Olivier shop, with its enticing choice of over two hundred cheeses from all over France, and huge slabs of different butters.

Further up the hill, the recently redundant town museum housed in a former convent, a 1730s mansion behind an imposing gateway, now has temporary exhibitions; almost opposite it, at No 113 Grande Rue, you may visit the Casa San Martin (open Sat-Wed 10–12/2–6), the home of the general who liberated his native Argentina, and also Chile and Peru, from Spanish rule in the early years of the nineteenth century. He spent the last years of his life here, exiled by Simon Bolivar, and there is a lively equestrian statue of him by Allouard, near the casino. Although somewhat primped up by the Argentine government, the house retains the atmosphere of a solid bourgeois town mansion of the 1840s.

Compact and tightly enclosed by thirteenth-century rectangular ramparts, pierced by massive gateways, the *Ville Haute* (upper town) crowns the summit of the hill, standing on a Roman site. According to Tobias Smollett, who described his stay in Boulogne in the eighteenth century, this was the aristocratic *quartier* of the town. Just outside the ramparts is a curious statue of 1881 by Alfred Jacquemart, with an Egyptian theme – Auguste Mariette, a local man, perched on a pyramid. He donated his collection of Egyptian antiquities to the local museum.

The imposing dome of the Italianate classical basilica of Notre Dame dominates the Ville Haute. It replaced the cathedral, destroyed after the Revolution, and was completed in 1866 to the design of Monsignor Haffreingue, its amateur architect. Domes are not easy to design, and it cannot be said that this one is entirely successful. All the same, Boulogne, a relatively small town, is fortunate to have such a lordly and idiosyncratic landmark. Although the interior is usually despised by architectural critics, the nave is a powerful space with its giant Corinthian pilasters. Below the dome is a splendid 1875 monument to Delaplanche, to the Monsignor, showing him offering a model of his design to the Virgin, who miraculously appeared here in the seventh century. The church has been celebrated ever since for its pilgrimage of Notre Dame de Boulogne, its importance mentioned by Chaucer. The elaborate marble high altar was executed in Rome at the expense of Prince Torlonia. There is a treasury of religious objects, but the essential visit is to the enormous and labyrinthine crypt: a succession of dimly lit vaulted chambers, some of them with fading mural paintings *en grisaille*, it makes an eerie experience. The *clou* is the remarkable Romanesque crypt with its painted pillars, where Edward II of England married Isabelle of France in 1303.

Lined with old houses, the quiet narrow streets of the *Ville Haute* are agreeable to wander about in. A quick detour may be taken through the Porte de Calais, adjoining the cathedral, to the nearby rue de la Porte Neuve: at No 5 is a 1930s *charcuterie* with jolly ceramic friezes and panels of all the ingredients running wild before being caught for the pot. In the main street, the rue de Lille, a shop offers an ingenious selection of marzipan sweets in the shape of animals and fish. The bakery opposite has kept its original interior, and there are other old-fashioned shops and a number of small restaurants nearby. In the cobbled main square – the Place de la Résistance – is the late neo-Classical Palais de Justice built in 1852, its sculpted tympanum by Bougron depicting Napoleon and Charlemagne, and the eighteenth-century Hôtel de Ville, built against the stocky thirteenth-century belfry tower. The ground floor of the Hôtel de Ville has been recently mundanely modernized, but on the first floor, the architect Colladent created a stylish 1950s scheme with his own large mural and an enormous wrought iron swan, the symbol of the town. The main reception rooms are the oak-panelled Salle de Mariage, the Salle de Fêtes with a huge painting by Jacquand showing the town refusing to surrender to Henry VIII of England at the siege of 1544 (but the siege was successful and Henry possessed the town for six years), and the Salle du Conseil with a number of portraits of famous locals and a huge canvas by Schommer depicting President Sadi Carnot's visit to Boulogne in 1889.

On the far side of the square is the Hôtel Desandrouins of 1777 by Giraud Sannier, where Napoleon stayed when planning his invasion of England and now somewhat grandiloquently called the Imperial Palace.

To the east, in the rue Aumont, attached to the Porte de Gayole, is a charming eighteenth-century fountain adorned with cherubs – the Fontaine des Amours. The most important feature of the *Ville Haute* is the massive château, an early example of a castle without a keep, built in the thirteenth century, and approached across a stone bridge and through an eighteenth-century gateway from the rue du Château, just east of the Basilica. Le Sage, author of the once popular novel *Gil Blas*, died in a house in this street. The château has an octagonal plan with round towers, it is built around a central courtyard, and was much altered in the eighteenth century. Recently well restored, it now houses the excellent Musée des Beaux-Arts et l'Archéologie. The collection includes a number of antiquities and important Greek vases, ceramics from the major French factories, and twentieth-century studio pottery. The paintings, although not exceptional, include works by Corot, Boudin, Delacroix and David of the nineteenth century, and modern paintings by, among others, Derain and Marquet.

Below the southern ramparts in the boulevard du Prince Albert, a series of monuments includes a massive bust of Henri II by David d'Angers, not one of his best works; the bronze and stone 1898 war memorial, called the Monument du Souvenir Français, by E. Lormier; and an 1865 memorial to Jenner, by the untalented Eugène Paul, erected in gratitude for the French lives saved by his celebrated vaccine.

Close to the D341, leading out of the town eastwards, is the large Cimitière Est. A number of Englishmen are buried there, including Richard Martin, founder of the RSPCA, who died in 1834. It also includes a trio of First World War memorials: one French, one English by Charles Holden, not here at his best, and a rather weird Portuguese structure.

A short excursion should be made to **Le Portel**, a former fishing port, now a small seaside resort attached to Boulogne, which was destroyed in the last war and rebuilt in the 1950s. This new town has a definite feeling of civic pride, being very spruce and well-kept, without the usual dead hand of so much post-war urban planning – probably because the architects maintained the old street pattern. The heart of the town is the main square, framed by quite effective modern terraces and shops and dominated by the excellent stone-faced post-war church of St Pierre & St Paul, with a parabolic

LE PORTEL: The Hôtel de Ville

arched interior in the manner of Gaudi, and highly effective stained glass by the distinguished artist Gabriel Loire. Nearby, in the trim park, is a bullet-holed war memorial. The second modern church, Ste Thérèse, to the south, is 1950s utilitarian, but with a facade enlivened by the eccentricity and economy of a painted-on rose window.

One of the few buildings to have survived the wartime destruction is the Hôtel de Ville by Bonhomme. Surprisingly grand and stylish for such a small town, it is a good quality Art Deco achievement of 1932, with excellent ironwork grilles and gates to the forecourt. There is no need to bother with the interior.

Boulogne: North Excursion

Wimereux and **Wimille** are just to the north of Boulogne, and indeed virtually attached to it. Wimereux is a proper seaside resort, with a good beach and many ornamental villas decorated with pictorial tile panels and evocative names, recalling both the Edwardian and the inter-war eras. One notable example, Le Sphinx, features tile panels of Egyptian figures and decorative details that could have come from Owen Jones's book, *The Grammar of Ornament*. In the cemetery is the grave of John McCrae, the Canadian author of the most famous poem of the Great War, 'In Flanders Fields'. There is a lively Mussels Festival in the summer. The ugly 1868 church of the Immaculate Conception contains post-war art such as the stations of the cross by Claude Gruer and stained glass in hot colours by Rocher and Lhotellier.

Across the railway to the east is Wimille, an older but altogether less appealing town, redeemed by the château of Lozembrune, built in the mid eighteenth-century post-Mansart classical style, with 1830s extensions. There are several memorials – commemorating, among other things, the first radio transmission by Marconi between France and England and Pilâtre de Rozier's unsuccessful attempt to cross the Channel in a hot air balloon in 1785 which ended in his death – but they are all dull. Much more

WIMEREUX: Lettering detail

impressive, south of the town, is the Colonne de la Grande Armée, 53 metres high, commenced in 1804 but not completed until 1841, and built of white local stone, to the designs of Eloi Labarre to commemorate the Napoleonic army which was assembled here for the planned invasion of Britain. With his back resolutely to England, the Emperor himself stands on top, a copy of the sculpture by Bosio (the 'French Canova'), permanently enjoying the views which can be shared by anyone prepared to climb the 263 steps to the platform below the statue. Napoleon was so confident of conquering England that he ordered a medal to be struck reading 'London 1804'.

Set into the side of the hill below the column is Terlincthun Military Cemetery. The approach is through an oak gate with stone piers, in a crisp Arts & Crafts style. Two pyramid-roofed classical stone pavilions stand on a balustraded terrace elevated above the rows of tombs. The design was by Leith and Hutton, under the supervision of Sir Herbert Baker, in a particularly restrained style which brings to mind Lutyens rather than Baker. The bodies of the dead who could be identified have their tombs inscribed accordingly, with their rank and regiment, while the others carry the traditional inscription, 'Known unto God', which was chosen by Rudyard Kipling, an adviser to the War Graves Commission. Some of the memorial stones are very recent – the bodies of First World War soldiers are still being discovered in the fields of northern France. And not only bodies; every week on the Front unexploded shells and poison gas containers come to the surface. It is estimated that several million shells remain for disposal. Terlincthun was the final stopping place in 1922 of George V and Queen Mary, on their pilgrimage of the Great War memorials then being constructed.

Boulogne: East Excursion

The inevitable hypermarkets and trading estates on the outskirts of Boulogne are abruptly left behind as one ventures into the Boulonnais, the home of a famous breed of shire horse used in the battle of Agincourt. This pretty and lightly populated landscape of rolling hills and woodland with a succession of attractive farming villages was used by Conan Doyle as the setting of several of his historical novels.

Start at **Souverain-Moulin**, where the rather hefty grey stone bulk of the eighteenth-century château is softened by the surrounding water and woodland. The chapel contains a 1952 tapestry by Jean Lurçat. The nearby village of **Pittefaux** has an enjoyable and old-fashioned air about it, which is shared by others in the area, notably **Belle** and **Le Wast**, further east. Particular pleasures are the old cafés, relics of pre-war France, and the many window-boxes that decorate the cottages in the summer. Pause at the Le Wast to admire the Romanesque doorway of the church of St Michel with its oriental mofits, probably inspired by a Crusader's travels. The splendid château at **Colembert** was built between 1777 and 1781 to the designs of Giraud Sannier; this monumental but elegant structure sits in a handsome landscaped park. It is not open to the public, but can be enjoyed from the main gates on the D252. An attractive and leisurely return route to Boulogne may be taken via the agreeable villages of **Alincthun, Bellebrune, Cremarest,** and **Wirwignies** (here, on the D341, a 1910 bronze monument depicts a lightly clad female weeping over the crashing racing car of Guippone).

THE BOULONNAIS: *A typical café exterior*

COLOMBERT: *The château*

MONTREUIL-SUR-MER: *The Caveé St Firmin*

Boulogne:
Excursion south along the N1

The old road south to Paris really begins at **Pont-de-Briques**, now little more than a roundabout encircling the modest château where Napoleon planned his campaign against the Austrians and fell out with his Empress Josephine. In the cemetery of the adjoining village of **St Etienne-au-Mont**, is a monument, vaguely oriental, to the Chinese Labour Corps who served in the Great War.

The N1 then passes an agreeable succession of small manors and old farms. To escape the hurtling lorries and the English tourists, take a short diversion to **Hesdigneul-lès-Boulogne** for the station hotel with its colourful, if battered, tiled facade and good lettering.

Pause at the small town of **Samer** (pronounced Sam-may), famous for its strawberries, with an annual festival in May. Its large and picturesque cobbled square, depicted by Sir William Russell Flint, is fringed with old houses and cafés, and dominated by the church, against which pantiled cottages huddle. The little white pedimented *bibliothèque* has the look of a prim English non-conformist chapel. The Mairie houses a dusty small museum with works by Jean-Charles Cazin, who was born here in 1841.

Now head southwards for 23 kms to **Montreuil-sur-Mer**. Despite its name, Montreuil is 17 kms inland – an indication of how much land has been reclaimed from the sea over the centuries. Once a port, with a monastery and a fortress, it was an important town in the Middle Ages, with some 40,000 inhabitants. Although its glory is now part of history, this is a walled hilltop town of great charm, overlooking the Canche valley and entered via narrow town gates that pierce its still extensive ramparts.

Seventeenth- and eighteenth-century houses line the winding cobbled streets, notably the steep and picturesque Cavée St Firmin which is often used as a film set, as in *Les Misérables* – Victor Hugo did in fact set part of his book in Montreuil. In the large and traditional main square, the place du Général de Gaulle, is a fine statue, by Paul Landowski, of Field Marshal Haig on his horse, Miss Ypres, in front of the theatre, which was converted from the old market-hall. Between 1916 and 1919 Haig lived at the Château de Beaurepaire, 4 kms to the south.

Montreuil is rich in military history, from the wars of the fourteenth century onwards. A most enjoyable walk is along the three kilometres of the old ramparts which completely enclose the town, and incorporate the citadelle, the deep moats of which are now dry, and are occasionally given over to unexpected activities like tennis. Mostly of the sixteenth and seventeenth century, the citadelle was built by Jean Errard de Bar-le-Duc, with later additions by Vauban. Its particular quality of peace and privacy has been shattered by the felling of the great elms that used to ornament it. Opposite, the château of Montreuil, behind its high wall, is uncannily like a country house by Lutyens. Its steep-pitched mellow tiled roofs with dormer windows, angled plan, massive brick chimney stacks, and green shuttered windows are all typically Lutyens. In the 1930s it belonged to an English playboy and amateur architect, Frank Wooster. He died on a world tour, but his rich and exotic Egyptian wife continued the tour, taking his coffin with her. The house is now, aptly, a luxurious hotel with a gastronomic reputation.

Trees are also a feature of the place d'Antal in the town centre. Limes shade a nineteenth-century cast iron fountain and a 1914–18 war memorial by Henri Gréber of an angel comforting a soldier, and lead in avenues towards the ancient abbey church of St Saulvé and the Flamboyant Gothic Chapel of the Hôtel Dieu which was much altered by Clovis Normand, a pupil of Viollet-le-Duc. The Mairie nearby has an attractive 1911 painting in the foyer, of the Cavée

MONTREUIL-SUR-MER: Statue of Field-Marshall Haig

St Firmin. The rue Delannoy continues to a little museum in the chapel at the end of the street, before leading into the rue du Clape-en-Bois with its pretty colour-washed cottages. The attractions of Montreuil have appealed to visitors, and particularly the English, since the eighteenth century. Lawrence Sterne stayed at the Hôtel de France, an old coaching inn which still welcomes visitors, and Sir Frank Brangwyn often painted in and around the town. Sensible English travellers will follow their example and make it their first proper stop after Boulogne.

In the avenue Général Leclerc, the road heading out of town towards Berck – there are some 1920s villas with a decided late Art Nouveau flavour. In a hamlet under the ramparts, **La Madeleine-sous-Montreuil**, there is a picturesque inn called the Auberge de la Grenouillère, a restaurant with rooms, much appreciated by the locals for its good food. Food apart, it should be visited for the rare taste of its interior, with good antique furniture and an old-fashioned fireplace with pretty blue Desvres tiles.

Montreuil is an ideal base for exploring the pretty river valleys of the region – particularly the Canche, with its trout and eels, its luxuriant landscape, and its profusion of old farms and manor houses.

Boulogne: South Coast

The coast road south of Boulogne, the D119, has little appeal, and the places it takes you to are unexciting. **Equihen-Plage**, once a haunt of artists is now just a collection of seaside bungalows and chalets – careless development exploiting a good beach. **Hardelot-Plage** is larger and rather more exclusive, with large white villas discreetly scattered among the pinewoods. The original layout was commissioned from Cordonnier. It has definite affinities with the better parts of Le Touquet, and indeed the English did much to encourage its development. The golf course was established in 1907 with the Duke of Argyll as its president. Today it is still known as a sporting resort, with golf and tennis as well as the obvious aquatic activities. New tower blocks of luxury apartments dominate the seafront, and new development has generally buried any remaining 1920s and 1930s architecture beneath a veneer of tasteless and affluent kitsch. If you can find your way through the maze of roads among the pine trees, try to reach **Condette**, (a village popular with the English including Charles Dickens) to see the curious 1850s Gothic castle built by an English magistrate, Sir John Mare, in a style that is very picturesque in its wooded setting. Incongruous in Northern France, it would look more at home on the Welsh borders. It was chosen by Roman Polanski to shoot scenes for his film 'Tess' (i.e. Tess of the d'Urbevilles).

CALAIS (Pas de Calais)

As Calais is the nearest French port to England it is inevitably the most familiar to the English, with Dover Castle only 38 kms away, and visible on clear days. A regular passenger boat service from England was established as long ago as 1821, with the steamboat Rob Roy. Calais was actually in English hands for over two hundred years until it was retaken by the French in 1558 – whereupon the much quoted saying of Mary Tudor that the name Calais would be found engraved on her heart after her death. For Winston Churchill, it was his "exotic port of entry into France" – meaning that he was en route for a painting holiday in the South of France. But it should be remembered that in 1940 Churchill gave the order to fight to the last man to defend Calais. The result of those three crucial days that May was that there were no escapees: they were all either killed or captured, but their sacrifice made the evacuation of Dunkerque possible. On the east side of the harbour, near where the ferries dock, is a monument to the heroism of the Green Jackets, with the traditional Cross of Sacrifice, which is on the site of their last stand.

Few of the nine million people who pass through each year do more than snatch a hurried meal or visit the hypermarket. Calais is the largest town of the *département* of Pas-de-Calais; war-battered and mostly rebuilt in a banal and cheap way, it seems to have little to detain the traveller on first sight, but is actually worth exploring. The old town, ringed by water, adjoins the port. On the quay is a long curved terrace of fishermen's housing with steep pantiled roofs, a Flemish version of the Arts and Crafts style. The striking external spiral staircases at the back are, however, very much of the 1950s. Nearby is an elegant stone Doric column, commemorating the return of Louis XVIII in 1814 ("fut rendu a l'amour des Français"), and the restoration of the monarchy in France, and a well sculpted 1899 monument by E. Lormier to the *sauveteurs* or

lifeboatmen. The place d'Armes, the main square and the old marketplace, was reconstructed with dull post-war concrete buildings. All that is left of the original medieval heart of the town, which was devastated in the last war, is the impressive thirteenth-century Tour du Guet, which served as a lighthouse until 1848. The modern lighthouse, visible over the roof tops, can be visited in summer for its excellent views. Just off the Place, in the main shopping street, the casino is indicative of local conservatism – its curved Dutch gable is as recent as 1950.

To the west is a prosperous *quartier*, well rebuilt in brick, where Emma, Lady Hamilton, Nelson's mistress, died in 1815 in poverty after fleeing a debtors' prison in England. Beau Brummel was also a resident exile while the pre-Raphaelite artist Ford Madox Brown was born in Calais. In 1802, in the lull of Anglo-French hostilities, Wordsworth spent a month here, in company with his sister Dorothy, in order to get to know his nine year old love-child by a Frenchwomen. They bathed in the sea and William wrote a sonnet – 'Calais 1802'.

Further to the west is the moated Citadelle, originally built after the English were driven out of Calais, and later remodelled by Vauban. It had unhappy memories for the architect Sir John Vanbrugh, who was incarcerated here in 1690 as a hostage in time of war. And in 1748, suspected of spying, William Hogarth was arrested for sketching the fortifications. It is now a well-tended place in which the locals exercise their dogs, and has a modern sports stadium, its serpentine roof demonstrating a stylish use of concrete.

Across the bridge which leads towards the sandy beach, next to Fort Risban, also remodelled by Vauban, is a swirly Art Nouveau monument by Guillaume (1913) on a roundabout, commemorating the catastrophic loss in the Channel of the French submarine Pluviôse in 1910 (named after one of the months of the Revolutionary calendar). Opposite is a monument

CALAIS: The towers of Notre Dame and the Hôtel de Ville and fishermens' houses fronting the port

CALAIS: The war memorial

to a local aviator, Brazy, who took part in the 1928 rescue by Amundsen of the Umberto Nobile North Pole expedition. Beyond, on the sandy beach, crowded with beach-huts, is a memorial to Captain Matthew Webb, the first man to swim the Channel, in 1875, covered in porpoise oil and taking just under twenty-two hours.

Back in the old town, the church of Notre Dame, where Charles de Gaulle married a local girl in 1921, is usually described as the only English Perpendicular church in France; one can only suppose this to mean that it was built during the period of the English occupation, since it is not particularly English in appearance. A closer inspection reveals an unusual Baroque oval chapel built in the 1630s at the east end, and a large stone walled cistern by Vauban, which acted as a reservoir in case of siege. Below the curious and very un-English tower, the sight of which always gave pleasure to Ruskin whenever he landed, is a massive stone north addition, almost worthy of Giles Gilbert Scott.

The modern Musée des Beaux Arts sometimes has good temporary exhibitions, and there is a worthwhile permanent collection of nineteenth and twentieth-century sculpture with works by Carpeaux, Dalou, Rodin, Epstein and Zadkine. The picture collection is entertaining if not exceptional, apart from works by English artists such as Bonington, who lived in Calais, and E.W. Cooke: usually only a small selection is shown. One very curious picture shows a beauty surrounded by her male admirers in bird form. A large section of the museum is devoted to lace – the principal nineteenth century industry of Calais which expanded thanks to three Nottingham lace-workers who, risking the death penalty in England, smuggled in looms in 1816. Lace is still an important local industry, but now concentrates on fashionable lingerie. The museum also includes an enormous and eye-catching scale model showing Calais as it was in 1904.

Crossing the George V bridge, one enters

CALAIS: Detail of the Pluviôse memorial

CALAIS: A detail of Rodin's **Burghers of Calais**

the nineteenth-century part of Calais known as St Pierre. Only too obvious is the immense 75-metre-high tower of the Hôtel de Ville, an idiosyncratic landmark for many miles around. Cordonnier and Guimard submitted schemes for the competition, but the lesser known Debrouwer was finally chosen. Work started in 1911 – hence the ponderous neo-Flemish design – but by the time of its completion in 1926 the Art Deco style had influenced the details of the tower which, although of brick and stone, has a reinforced concrete frame. The allegorical figures are by Jules Desbois. The interior should be visited to admire the quality of the craftmanship of the excellent wrought iron, the mosaic work and murals upstairs, and a stained-glass window depicting the 1347 siege of the town. In the lobby a small showcase exhibits the Légion d'Honneur and two Croix de Guerre et Palme awarded to the city for valour during World War II. The bronze busts in the main lobby are of the Duc de Guise, who recaptured Calais from the English, and Cardinal Richelieu.

In the square in front of the Hôtel de Ville is the justifiably famous sculpture by Rodin of the Burghers of Calais, which movingly recalls the humiliation of Calais by Edward III after his victory over the French at Crécy. Destined for execution in lieu of the destruction of the town, the six hostages, leading local citizens, were spared by the pleas of Edward's wife. It is odd that the town should have erected an Hôtel de Ville of such a conservative design after

commissioning this *avant garde* work, which took albeit ten years to complete, amid some controversy. It was finally unveiled in 1895. It is interesting to compare the Rodin with the flamboyant and much more conventional Art Nouveau monument of the same period to French deeds of valour, which is in the park opposite. The park also contains the Musée de la Guerre, housed in a former Nazi blockhouse and communications centre, a permanent and sinister reminder for the citizens of the reality of the last war. In a series of claustrophobic rooms, a collection of wartime relics and photographs illustrates the scale of the destruction of the town. The stark external lines are fortunately relieved by the surrounding greenery, and the cheerful and decorative cast-iron fountain nearby. The remainder of Calais is of conventional mainly nineteenth-century build, with a good shopping centre. The only notable building, on the main cross-roads, is the grandiose but now rather down-at-heel theatre of 1905, with alluring ladies adorning the facade which represent the muses (by Paul Graf and E. Lormier). In front of this is a monument of 1910 by Marius Roussel to Jacquard, the inventor of the well-known loom which bears his name – here surrounded by simpering girls. In the rue Pascal, the dull exterior of the 1924 church of St Joseph conceals some rather striking Art Deco stained glass and mural painting by Louis Barillet. On the southern outskirts of the town, on the N1 to Dunkerque will be found the Cimetière Sud which incorporates a British Military cemetery with stone pavilions designed by Leith under Sir Herbert Baker.

On the western outskirts of the town, close to the N1, stands the ancient Fort Nieulay, rebuilt by Vauban and recently restored. It once guarded the sluice gates which were opened to flood the hinterland when Calais was under attack.

Calais is under a new form of attack with the construction of the Channel Tunnel to the west of the town. Margaret Thatcher and President Mitterand signed an agreement in 1986 to launch this vast project. No one is absolutely sure what the future holds for Calais, but as a focal point between London, Paris and Brussels, with fast direct connections by rail and motorway and a promised 46 million travellers en route each year, changes are inevitable. A huge multinational shopping centre is already planned on the outskirts of the town. Will the hordes ever linger in the town, thus surely changing its character, or will they just pass through?

Calais: West Coast Excursion

An enjoyable alternative to the busy N1 south from Calais is the D940 coast road south-west from Calais, for it offers a number of attractions. But first the Calais suburbs spread to **Blériot-Plage**, where the dunes and the chalets take over. Louis Blériot, the first cross-Channel aviator, is commemorated in a most inadequate fashion. Far better served is the memory of Blériot's unsuccessful rival, Latham (a Frenchman despite his name), marked by a particularly nonchalant statue of a cheery chap with his scarf blowing in the wind at **Cap Blanc Nez**. He stands on the wind-swept cliffs, which are pock-marked with small craters from wartime shell attacks.

On the way to the Cap, one passes the entrance to the Channel Tunnel, under construction at **Sangatte**. Between this village, and those of Coquelles and Fréthun, some 800 hectares are being developed for the new terminal which is due for completion in 1993. 'At last!' one may say; it has been proposed so many times over the past three centuries, but now it seems to be a reality. An exhibition centre illustrates the scheme, the costliest ever privately financed building project.

Cap Blanc Nez offers marvellous views across the Channel to England and also over the sandy beaches and the coast-line in both directions, especially from the tall obelisk of the Dover Patrol Memorial, to the minesweepers who kept the Channel clear.

The next stop is the little resort of **Wissant**, which has its own particular seaside atmosphere, and some eccentric houses one, now derelict, has a Norman tower, while another is in the Egyptian style. This little place was reputedly a Channel port in the ninth century, but now there are just a few fishing boats, some casually parked in the main square. **Cap Gris Nez** is a disappointment, consisting of some holiday chalets, a lighthouse and radar station, and a landscape far duller than that at Cap Blanc Nez. The coast and the fields behind are scattered with the remains of old blockhouses and fortifications, part of the Atlantic Wall which the Germans started building in 1940. Some have been put to use as tractor sheds and one, at Audinghen, is now a war museum, the Musée 39/45 devoted to the Atlantic Wall, housed in the former Battery Todt, which once contained a 380 mm gun used to shell Dover. Fritz Todt, the engineer responsible for Germany's autobahns in the 1930s, headed the organisation which employed over two million deportees as labour for the Nazi wartime constructions. It is arranged rather haphazardly with a good many guns, uniforms, propaganda posters and other souvenirs of the war. Its lack of spruce display evokes something of life in a bunker in 1942. If this is to your taste there is another wartime site to be visited, 12 kms to the east, at **Landrethun-le-Nord**, where there is another blockhouse museum, the Forteresse de Mimoyecques, devoted to Hitler's final fling, the V–3 London rocket, projected to destroy London. East of **Marquise**, marble and granite have been quarried since Roman times, and provide a third of national production. A museum illustrates the history of marble quarrying. **Audinghen** is an essential visit for lovers of the bizarre, for the truly eccentric church of St Pierre built in 1960, and designed by a local man, Antoine Colladant; it looks as though it was run up by some local builder on the basis of a rough sketch by Le Corbusier on the back of a menu after a heavy lunch. Its most obvious feature, dominating the skyline, is a detached tower in the form of a giant lyre, surmounted by a cockerel. The sloping roof is painted in blue and white; the curved porch, with its heavenly message in stained glass letters, leads to an interior with some extraordinary stained glass. Much of the decoration was the work of Geneviève d'Andreis, who also produced the mosaic memorial beside the road to the south of the village.

Another curious place is **Amblctcuse**, 5 kms further on, a little town that once knew greater days as a port of some significance. Standing in the sea, just off the beach, is Vauban's Fort Mahon, built to protect the harbour, which was used by Napoleon to moor part of his invasion fleet. Earlier, James II, fleeing England, arrived here in 1689. Today there are quiet streets of decaying seaside villas, old tiled shopfronts, and, in the rue du Fort, some garages with a tiled frieze of early racing cars.

Calais: South East Excursion

A pleasant road, the D127, leads from Calais to **Guînes**, and runs alongside a canal, marked by a series of Dutch-style bascule bridges and a variety of those ingeniously-patterned concrete palisade fences favoured by the French.

Guînes itself is an agreeable little town with many single-storey cottages, a typical large main square with pretty 1930s lettering on the Restaurant Lion d'Or, and a monument commemorating François de Guînes, who liberated the town in 1558 from two hundred years of English domination. Just outside Guînes, on the road towards Ardres, is a granite monolith standing in an unchanging agricultural landscape. This marks the site of the Field of the Cloth of Gold where the two young rival monarchs, François I and Henry VIII met in 1520 with a view to forming an alliance to counter the threat to France from Charles V, Emperor of Austria, who held the Low Countries. It was a sumptuous occasion, each king vying with the other in a display of extravagance. François' tent was embroidered with gold, and decorated by the painter Jean Bourdichon. In the event it all went rather wrong, particularly for Henry. His crystal palace blew away, and his pride was damaged by a fall during the jousting, so no one was really surprised when the planned *entente cordiale* came to nothing.

South of the town, pretty roads penetrate the forest of Guînes, where a marble column marks the spot at which Blanchard and Jeffries, a British doctor, landed in 1785 having made the first successful hot air balloon crossing of the Channel.

Continue along the D231 and you soon come to **Ardres**, an agreeable little town with a triangular cobbled main square, the place d'Armes, where the fine church of Notre-Dame-de-Grace and St Omer makes the main impact. Richard II of England married Isabelle of France here in 1395, a century before destruction of the town by English troops. The church was rebuilt in 1503–20 and this is what we see today, though there was a heavy-handed restoration in 1877. Nearby is the Carmelite chapel built in 1679. The surrounding streets have a pleasing old-fashioned air – the *maison de la presse* has an excellent cast-iron shop front, and one can wander among the pleasant lime avenues planted in the eighteenth century or visit the verdant grounds of the mairie – a last breath of rural France before catching the ferry. During the First World War there were many British training camps and depots here and if you look carefully you can still find traces of the network of trenches created to give soldiers practical experience before going to the Western Front.

From Ardres take the D224 north-east to **Nortkerque**, a small farming village with a certain appeal. Its most unexpected feature is the church, the tower of which is like an oversized Art Deco clock. Inside, the strong late eighteenth-century columns contrast with vivid stained glass and mosaic panels in a seaside villa, or 1930s Odeon, style. The war memorial, not for once to the Great War, has an 1870 low-relief bronze panel of angels and children, and also commemorates an 1859 campaign in Italy.

The road now leads to **Audruicq**. It is best to come here on Wednesdays when the market fills the large central square, at one end of which there is a war memorial (not a very successful composition); there is also a plaque describing in considerable detail the liberation of the town by the Canadians in 1944. An 1887 house features cast-iron work and decorative tiling. It is worth taking the road on from here to **Zutkerke** where, just outside the town, a very singular 1920s villa stands by the roadside. The gate is a vigorous display of wrought-iron crafts-manship, and the house itself, peach-coloured and vaguely Viennese in style, features bright ceramic tile panels and friezes of swans, chickens and other domestic animals.

CAMBRAI (Nord)

Despite the ravages of the British bombardment of 1917 and mining by the Germans in retreat in 1918, this small Flemish city has great character. As was so often the case in the north, textiles were the basis of the city's wealth, including the fine linen that we call cambric, but the importance of agriculture always ensured that Cambrai never became a heavily industrialised town. An English equivalent might be Hereford. There is plenty to enjoy. Stone town mansions of the seventeenth and eighteenth-centuries line cobbled streets,

such as the rue de l'Epée in which the Musée Municipal is housed in an eighteenth-century hotel, set back behind high walls and a large cobbled courtyard. After years of neglect the museum is now in the hands of an enthusiastic curator and is being reorganised. The collections of French and Flemish paintings are good, but the sculpture is of particular interest, with medieval carvings from the old cathedral, seventeenth-century work by Balthazar Marsy, and, at the foot of the stairs, E.J. Carlier's huge, sensual sculpture of 1897, 'Le Miroir': a handsome female nude in white marble is attended by a black maidservant, in bronze but ingeniously draped in marble. Also sensual is the beguiling sculpture of 1889 – 'Sappho Endormie', by Marguerite Syamour, whose talent ought to be better known.

The eighteenth-century cathedral of Notre Dame, a typical example of northern classicism, though somewhat restored, has some very effective *trompe l'oeil* panels painted *en grisaille* in 1760 by Martin Geeraerts of Antwerp, as well as a highly romantic monument by David d'Angers (1824), to François de Salignac de la Mothe-Fénelon, better known as Fénelon, the writer and Archbishop of Cambrai. Two important composers of early music, du Faÿ and Josquin des Prés, were respectively music-master and choir-master of the old cathedral.

Facing the cathedral, a very odd monument to Fénelon stands in front of the Jesuit chapel of 1694, with its swirling theatrical Baroque facade with a relief of the Assumption, and nearby is the lop-sided Maison Espagnole, a late medieval but heavily restored timber-framed structure. Also in view is the solid but dull fourteenth-century Porte de Paris. Far more interesting is the huge and well-kept church of St Géry which contains, among many good things, a huge painting by Rubens, some excellent eighteenth-century woodwork and a splen-did Baroque rood screen in richly contrasting marbles by local sculptors, the Marsy brothers.

CAMBRAI: The Hôtel de Ville

CAMBRAI: Monument to Fénelon by David d'Angers

CAMBRAI: The war memorial

In the square adjoining St Géry, stands a gateway to the former archbishop's palace, sculpted in 1625 by Gaspard Marsy in a Flemish Mannerist style which would be quite at home in Antwerp. A few yards to the south, in a small triangular place recently renamed place Salvador Allende, a good sculpture of an androgynous angel by Hiolle, commemorates the 1870–71 Franco-Prussian war in an unusually unheroic fashion. Just east of St Géry, in the place du Neuf-Octobre, a tablet records the town's gratitude to the Canadians who liberated Cambrai in 1918, and a charming sculpture of a mother suckling a baby commemorates without explanation, a local worthy Edmond Garin.

The main square, the place Aristide Briand, is flanked by the grand formal classical facade of the Hôtel de Ville, originally designed in 1786 by the royal architect J.D. Antoine. It was rebuilt in 1874 by Guillaume, broadly retaining Antoine's design, with the pediment sculpted by E.E. Hiolle and later repaired after war damage. It has been recently cleaned and has a handsome bell tower flanked by blackamoors, Martin and Martine, who strike the hours. Inside, there are excellent frescoes in the lobby of Peace, Love and Work, and in the Salle de Mariage is an historical pageant; they are all by Emile Flamant (1930).

The tall and distinctive 70 metre high belfry tower in the mail St Martin to the south, is all that remains of the church of St Martin.

The place de la République, to the north, is rewarding for two good 1920s buildings, the Chambre de Commerce and the Crédit Agricole, both featuring low-relief carved panels of some quality. To the north, the Porte Notre Dame is an impressive gateway of 1623, with bold diamond-pointed rusticated stonework, a vestige of the old town fortifications. A few yards east of the main street, the avenue de la Victoire, is a rare delight: the Art Nouveau *charcuterie* in the rue des Liniers is complete and original, together with its handsome 1920s marble

CAMBRAI: *Jesuit chapel of 1694*

counters, and it is a pleasure to buy the ingredients for a good picnic, surrounded by pretty tiles decorated with swallows and morning glories with an ornate pink glass chandelier overhead. The exterior has its original woodwork and etched glass. To complete your picnic, buy your bread from the Art Nouveau *boulangerie* in the rue des Feutriers. In the rue St Georges, there is a distinguished eighteenth-century town house with gilded balconies at No 11. To the north-east is a medley of buildings: the 1950s covered market faces old Flemish houses, and nearby is a nineteenth-century brewery with an octagonal tower.

The beautifully kept public garden, le Jardin Public, extends to 22 hectares, unusually large for such a small town. It was laid out late in the nineteenth century, after the military had relinquished the ramparts. Among the trees are monuments and sculpture; bronze panels by Descatoire commemorate civil and military victims of the 14–18 War, a nearby panel records the epic tank battle of 20 November 1917, and there is an eccentric tribute of 1910 to the local aviator Blériot by André Laoust, with a bronze portrait by Carlier. Of higher artistic quality, are bronzes of mythological subjects: 'Gilliatt' by E-J Carlier, and 'Sarpedon' and 'Orpheus and Cerberus' both by Henri Peinte. The charming nude in stone – 'Pomona' – is by A.A. Pommier. For no obvious reason, one of the paths is named after Henry Moore. At the north end of the park is a massive stone 1914–18 war memorial: a dynamic mass of forceful soldiers and figures attached to a tank-like form, surprisingly unsigned. To the east of the park is the Citadelle, somewhat hidden by trees and now merely defending the banal buildings of the local tax office. The best feature is the Porte Royale, a fine gateway of 1623. At the northern edge of the town, the château de Selles is a more imposing military edifice.

LOUVERAL: The Memorial to the Missing

Cambrai: South Excursion

Leaving Cambrai by the Bapaume road, the N30, one soon reaches **Fontaine-Notre-Dame**, a village on the main road distinguished by its church of St Martin. The spire, a 1928 pierced concrete affair, has enormous cast low-relief panels set into its flanks. Inside, the 1980 stained glass sits rather unhappily with the rather good Arts and Crafts painted decoration. A diversion must then be made to the village of **Sauchy-Lestrée**, 8 kms north-west, where the church of St Aubert of 1931–33 is a rare example of the Expressionist style, by Léon Tissier of Paris. A powerful, compressed, pyramidal brick tower, on a stone plinth, encloses a tall entrance archway, angularly recessed to frame a huge stained glass Christ on the Cross by Jean Gaudin. Inside is a feature which may be unique: moulded glass stations of the cross executed by the famous Parisian glass maker René Lalique, to the designs of the Parisian sculptor Henri Bouchard. After

VILLERS-PLOUICH: The church

82

LOUVERVAL: The Memorial to the Missing: one of C.S. Jagger's panels

this excitement, the commemorative stained glass windows by Raphael Lardeur, commissioned by locals, might seem almost tame, good though they are.

Now head south-westwards to **Louverval**, where the Memorial to the Missing sits beside the N30. An awkward site has been mastered by Chalton Bradshaw, whose powerful unadorned classicism is relieved by two outstanding carved panels by C.S. Jagger: with their subtle blend of linear detail and deep relief, these must be among the best examples of British sculpture in the North of France. It was completed in 1930. Jagger won the Military Cross in France in 1918, but it was the horror of action at Gallipoli, where he was wounded, which resolved him to record in sculpture his experience. A small cemetery is set on a lower level, but linked to the memorial visually by clever landscaping.

From Louverval, go across country in a south-easterly direction, crossing the Canal du Nord in a dramatic deep cutting, busy with barges. There is a rather bizarre 1920s church at **Villers-Plouich**, the tower of which supports an enormous figure of Christ in Majesty, flatly carved in a rural Art Deco style. A war memorial of similar style stands nearby. Cross over the A26 motorway to the N44. A minor road leads across the St Quentin canal, with its pretty lockkeeper's lodge, to the ruined abbey of **Vaucelles**. Founded in 1131, this Cistercian abbey housed over 400 monks and brothers at its peak in the thirteenth century. Today there is still much to see: the massive vaulted barns, some recently restored, and the picturesque ruins of the huge seventeenth-century dormitory, a great classical pile overlooking the quiet valley of the Escaut.

A short diversion may be made to the north to **Masnières**, which has a striking war memorial by the canal bridge, a 1920s public building with an Art Nouveau-ish mask, and another Newfoundland caribou memorial.

Continue south along the N44 – pausing, if you wish, to see the dull remains of another abbey at **Gouy**. Near the source of the Escaut is the major American Cemetery at **Bony** and

BELLICOURT: *The American war memorial chapel and cemetery*

the American Memorial at **Bellicourt**, both of which commemorate the battles of September and October 1918, when the U.S. 27th and 30th divisions pierced the Hindenberg Line. A massive cenotaph by Harnon, the memorial is decorated with symbolic figures in a 1920s neo-Classical style, and has a table of orientation behind it, which provides a useful guide to the later battles of the Somme. Even more impressive is the chapel at Bony: decorated with flags and eagles and low-relief panels of guns, shells and tanks – the modern equivalents of classical military trophies – and with some interesting stained glass, this massive block-like structure in immaculate white stone stands guard over a field of marble crosses, meticulously arranged and maintained. Deep below the cemetery is the seven kilometre-long canal tunnel, built between 1802 and 1810, and converted by the Germans during

ESNES: The château

the First World War into an impenetrable fortress at the heart of the defensive Hindenberg Line.

The N44 now leads south to St Quentin, but if you return northwards cross country to **Esnes**, on the D960, there is a splendid fortified château, entered through a powerful and ornamental seventeenth-century gateway. It has been inhabited by the same family for twenty-nine generations and has endured many tribulations. Towers, barns, a dovecote and a dried-up moat complete the scene, now delightfully domestic.

The tour continues to **Caudry**, a reasonably pleasant lace-making town with a big central square, worth visiting for its war memorial by Paul Theunissen (1922): sturdy heroic figures and an angel holding a dying *poilu*, are set on a plinth with accomplished low-relief bronze panels depicting the German occupation, the rigours of war, and the relief of the town by the English.

To the east is **Le Cateau-Cambrésis**, a cheerful small Flemish town with a stormy past. Frequently besieged in the Middle Ages, it gained some peace and prosperity after Henri II of France signed a treaty here in 1559 with Philip II of Spain and Queen Elizabeth of England (who ceded Calais). Destroyed by French troops in 1642, it finally became a part of France in 1678. The Austrians occupied it in 1793, and the Russians in 1814. In this century both world wars caused some damage. On the way into the town, by the N43/D932 cross-roads, are two cemeteries: one is British, and the other is German – with a pyramidal memorial commemorating, unusually, both the French and the Germans.

In the centre, the elegant 1705 belfry by Jacques Nicolas de Valenciennes rises high above the seventeenth-century Hôtel de Ville and overlooks a small square with a lively 1838 statue of Mortier, one of Napoleon's marshals, by the Douai sculptor Bra, standing before a mosaic-fronted *charcuterie*. The main street slopes from here down to the archbishop's palace – the plain eighteenth-century Palais Fénelon, with its attractive park, reputedly landscaped by Le Nôtre. The palace now houses the Musée Henri Matisse. The great artist was born in Le Cateau in 1869, and before his death in 1954 he gave a collection of his works to the town – not major items, but well displayed and highly enjoyable. Also in the museum are works by the local Cubist, Auguste Herbin – in particular a colourful painted piano. Herbin is also responsible for a large mosaic on the facade of a modern school in the place 3 Septembre. Not far away is the dramatic Baroque facade, sculpted by Gaspard Marsy, of the Jesuit church of St Martin of 1634, now a little the worse for wear. The interior is made gloomy by some dreary post-war stained glass. You should particularly seek out the local infant school, the Ecole Maternelle Matisse, where a large stained glass window by the master in bright primary colours, casts a glowing light on small children at play. It is called 'Les Abeilles' (the Bees) and is one of his last works. A bust of Matisse stands outside. There is a military section in the municipal cemetery, with a most unusual multinational memorial of German origin.

Now take the N43 eastwards and cross the Canal de la Sambre. Near the canal, in the closing days of the Great War, the poet Wilfred Owen was machine-gunned to death soon after winning the Military Cross. He lies buried at **Ors**, 2 kms to the north of the N43 (in the Communal cemetery, *not* the British cemetery). At **Chapeau-Rouge** crossroads there is a small memorial to the First Division and the battles of August 1914, with an excellent bronze by Richard Goulden, an enlarged version of his memorial outside St Michael's, Cornhill, in the City of London.

DESVRES (Pas de Calais)

With its pottery factories, artisans' terraces and smoke drifting over the streets in the early morning, Desvres has more than

DESVRES: Interior of the Café de la Gare

DESVRES: Exterior of a tile factory

VALLEY OF THE COURSE: Farmhouse and ford at Doudeauville

VALLEY OF THE COURSE: The dépôt de tabac at Estrée

a faint echo of Stoke-on-Trent. A centre of pottery since the eighteenth century, but with traditions extending back to the Romans, Desvres still produces its traditional blue and white kitchen tiles, as well as reproducing the classic faiences of Rouen, Delft, Strasbourg, Moustiers, Nevers and elsewhere. This is a pity, for the results are inevitably sterile and boring. A visit to the so-called museum in the Hôtel de Ville brings this home forceably (it is however due to be expanded in 1991, one hopes for the better). But, do not despair, for Desvres and its surroundings are full of its most original product, decorative wall tiles. Desvres tiles can be seen on the fronts of houses and shops all over northern France, and there are some classic examples in the town itself. A panel advertising a butcher's shop can be seen near the church, and another, showing pottery workers stoking the kilns, is on the wall of the most famous tile factory, Fourmaintraux & Delassus – in the hands of the same family for nine generations, and one of several establish-

ments in the town whose workshops may be visited by appointment. Their wares on show these days are mundane but in the 1920s they supplied much ceramic decoration for the restoration of war-damaged churches. Tile enthusiasts should also make sure they visit two cafés with extensive tiling schemes – La Parisiana in the main square, which features landscape and agricultural scenes, and the Café de la Gare, near the station, with its ample Art Nouveau-ish maidens framed in flowery bowers. Tuesday is a good day to visit Desvres with all the animation of the livestock market, local produce squawking, mooing and baaing. A trip on a tourist train is available at summer weekends from Desvres, by a pretty route via Samer to Boulogne.

Desvres: South Excursion

South from Desvres, the D127 winds its way along the valley of the Course, which starts as a little stream and gradually develops into a substantial river, flowing through water meadows, with long avenues of poplars and trout farms. This is rural France as one always imagines it: a series of pretty farming villages set in the valley, fields broken up by patches of woodland, and animals scattered over the hillsides. The villages are essentially traditional, predominantly brick, wattle and daub and half-timbered, with only the enormous tractors linking them firmly, and noisily, to the present. At **Doudeauville** there is a splendid brick fortified farm dated 1613, approached across a ford, while at **Inxent** the pretty Auberge d'Inxent is a delightful inn, and a good halt for a meal in an old fashioned interior. A couple of churches deserve a glance: St Quentin at **Montcavrel**, with its bold silhouette, and St Omer at **Estrée**, where the carved doorway is primitive rural Baroque. An old *depôt de tabac* opposite is set in a courtyard, with a little dovecot attached to its side. These form a wonderful French scene, straight from some 1930s film. In the field beyond a family of extraordinary spotted horses wander among the poplars.

Another road from Desvres, the D108, runs south-eastwards to Hesdin. This is not so much an excursion as part of an attractive route from Calais to avoid the main roads, crossing broad plains and swooping down into steep-sided river valleys dotted with pretty Picardy villages of white walled cottages with orange pantiled roofs. One curiosity is the chapel on the hill south of **Embry** which looks as if it had been designed by a specialist in Edwardian bandstands.

DOUAI (Nord)

Douai is elegant and attractive and belies its proximity to the coal-mines and the industrial belt. Its aristocratic past was evoked by Balzac and some of its fine eighteenth-century architecture is still in evidence, despite severe war damage which destroyed over five hundred houses. The town has a solid provincial air today which partly stems from the weighty presence of the legal profession, Louis XIV, having secured Douai for France in 1713, made it the seat of the Flemish local government, the Parlement de Flandre, which was succeeded by the Court of Appeal after the Revolution. Earlier, Douai became a centre for English Catholics fleeing Queen Elizabeth I's oppression – hence the Douai Bible.

The town broadly retains its old street pattern, and there are a number of good eighteenth-century facades enlivened by decorative carved details: masks, amorini, statues and ornate window and door frames. A notable example is the Hôtel du Dauphin (now the tourist office) in the main square, the Place d'Armes. The square is not improved by recent tricksy landscaping, but it is well enclosed by a variety of urbane 1920s buildings, such as the Palace Cinema and the Villa Toriani. In view from the square, is the mighty medieval belfry, a noble model for all those created after the Great War. As the subject of a familiar painting by Corot, in the Louvre, and from its description by Victor Hugo, it is probably the best known in the North. Towering majestically above the Hôtel de Ville, it houses a famous carillon which plays surprising tunes. Within the Hôtel de Ville, a monumental staircase leads to the Salle de Mariage, with imported Louis XV panelling of some quality, and the exalted Salle Gothique of 1463 – a fine space indeed, though the date should read c.1900, when a romantic fantasy of the medieval period was created, with a high heavily beamed ceiling, linenfold panelled doors in ogival frames and a big carved stone fireplace, old but imported. Gorguet painted murals of courtly life, illuminated by fifty splendid bronze candelabra – a perfect setting for a costume drama.

North of the Place d'Armes, an animated shopping street, the rue de Bellain leads into the rue de la Madeleine. The Baroque dome of the church of St Pierre rises above mellow tiled roofs. The Art Deco Café Metropole faces the old fashioned Brulerie,

DOUAI: The Place d'Armes and the Hôtel de Ville

DOUAI: The war memorial

from which usually wafts the delicious smell of roasting coffee. Passing the smart 1930s marble facade of Decroix, turn left to reach the church of St Pierre. This immense, mainly eighteenth-century building is better than other guides acknowledge. The interior is a dramatic and well-proportioned space with much good craftsmanship, notably the ironwork, the flamboyant carved organ case, some interesting monuments and some 1930s stained glass. An unexpected feature is a series of dramatic low-relief marble panels depicting the massacre of the monks of St Amand – at first glance seemingly of the neo-Classical period, but actually dated 1689. The big square church tower is a pleasing amalgam of Gothic and Baroque ornament.

Around the corner, in the rue Bellegambe, is an outrageous and rare Art Nouveau shop front, flaunting flying curves and sunflowers, a wonderfully incongruous survival. Just nearby, in the rue des Ferronniers, is a more sober Art Nouveau facade by H. Sirot.

Due east of the Place d'Armes, hurriedly passing the banal post-war rebuilding, the rue de Valenciennes brings you to the attractive old church of Notre Dame, restored after war damage, with modern stained glass. Opposite, in a small park, the war memorial by Alexandre Descatoire is a strange mix of styles – a 1920s female angel, in front of a pointed arch is flanked by two powerful warrior figures, one in medieval dress with a crossbow, the other an over-stylised modern soldier. The lettering is curiously archaic. The large eighteenth-century building in the background is the Hôpital Général commenced in 1756 (which is early in that era when concern for public health led to an expansion of hospital building). At the east end of the church, a weedy statue by Bouquillon of the very popular poetess, Marceline Desbordes-Valmore, faces the beautifully wooded Parc Bertin and the ancient Porte Valenciennes, isolated on a roundabout.

West of the town centre, passing the Louis XV Hôtel d'Aoust, with its rococo details in the rue de la Comédie, there are agreeable walks along the quays of the river Scarpe. Agreeable that is, until one experiences the rude shock of the 1972 extension of the Palais de Justice. Will this monstrous multi-storey box ever achieve aesthetic appreciation? There is no problem, however, with the Palais itself, by Lequeux of Lille and dated 1762. The Grand'Chambre of this former seat of the Flemish parliament is elegantly appointed with panelling, wrought-iron work and wall paintings. To the north-west, in the rue des Chartreux, an important attraction of Douai is the Musée Municipal which is housed in a former monastery, the Ancienne Chartreuse, a pretty brick building in a delicate northern Renaissance style; it boasts a collection of high quality which is well displayed and includes Flemish, Dutch and French Old Master paintings, including work by Jean Bellegambe, who was born in Douai in 1470. Look out for an unattributed English eighteenth-century portrait – perhaps an over-looked Gainsborough? Another local artist was the sculptor Jean de Boulogne, born in 1524, who emigrated to Florence and is now better known as Giambologna. His *oeuvre* is unexpectedly represented here by 'Le Pissatore', a grinning Mannerist cherub gripping an grotesque mask where his stomach should be, and he is commemorated by a powerful early twentieth-century bronze by Descatoire, Rodinesque in style, which stands on a roundabout where the N43 from Cambrai enters the town.

Amateurs of good 1950s architecture should seek out the Bibliothèque Municipale, just off the rue de la Fonderie. The facade has a huge and effective sculpture by Morlaix. The nearby Conservatoire of 1959 has sculpture by Bouquillon, still in a pre-war tradition. Both buildings were designed by M. Coasnes, and are particularly enjoyable and animated when the pupils depart at the end of the day.

Those with an interest in folklore should turn up on the first Sunday after 5 July to

DOUAI: Art Nouveau shop front in the rue Bellegambe

see the Gayant festival and procession, with its vast medieval giants. The important local production of garlic is celebrated at an annual fair at **Arleux**, south of the town, an opportunity to sample a local speciality, garlic soup.

North-west of Douai, just south of **Oignies**, is a fine industrial landscape of canals and mines, which can be viewed from the Lille-Paris motorway. There is a good example where the motorway crosses the Canal de la Haute Deûle, an impressive industrial building, proudly labelled 'Charbons d'Oignies'. The largest steam engine in Europe, constructed at Oignies in 1930, is currently being restored and will be the focal point of a proposed museum – le Musée de la Mine et Chemin de Fer.

There is also an important mining museum, the Centre Historique Minière, at an actual colliery at **Lewarde**, 10 kms south-east of Douai, a centre of mining for over 250 years. The reality of life at the coal-face is very realistically presented.

DOULLENS: The entombment in the church of Notre Dame

DOULLENS (Somme)

With some industry on its outskirts, this small town in the valley of the Authie largely retains its traditional street pattern, with a number of eighteenth-century houses in the characteristic style of this part of Picardy, built of white limestone dressed with brick, with dormer windows. Macaroons are the local speciality.

Doullens is dominated by its unusually large old Citadelle, modified by Jean Errard de Bar-le-Duc, and later by Vauban, which stands on an eminence on the south-west outskirts of the town. Battered by time and by the battles between the French and the Spanish, the fortifications are somewhat delapidated, but are being restored.

The church of Notre Dame, in the centre of the town, has suffered damage in all the many conflicts of the last five hundred years and its exterior is frankly unprepossessing. Albert Roze was responsible for the sculpture in the porch, dated 1903, which is in the Gothic tradition but tinged by the then prevailing Art Nouveau taste. The interior is an essential visit (keys nearby at No 2 rue pont à Lavoine), to see its particularly beautiful Entombment of 1583, carved in a startlingly white limestone. The seven life-size figures gazing upon the body of Christ are richly attired in Renaissance dress, although the sepulchre is still Gothic in style. Church art of the twentieth-century includes stations of the cross carved in stone in 1954, by a monk of the abbey of Solesmes, Father Claude Gruer, a handsome font carved by Lamotte in 1957, stained glass windows by le Chevalier, and a large painting behind the altar by Cracco of 1930.

In the main street, the rue du Bourg, the quite modest Belfry, built in 1613 of pink brick with stone rustication, is set into the street frontage and is not the usual massive detached structure. The Musée Lombart, containing a hodge-podge of sculpture, paintings and ceramics (open Wednesdays, Saturdays and Sundays: 3 – 6) is housed in quite a grand building guarded by sphinxes, which was built in 1908 by M. Lombart, a chocolate manufacturer. The pretty garden, planted *à la française*, is adorned with sculpture including a bronze by Maillard.

Set in a little park on a hillside to the south is a calvary which includes a powerful head of Foch, modelled by Albert Roze in 1921, a reminder of the conference held in the grandiose Hôtel de Ville of Doullens on 26 March 1918, at which Haig accepted the appointment of Foch as Supreme Commander of the Allied Forces. This decision was vital to the ultimately successful resistance to the German offensive of 1918, and thus to the outcome of the war. The conference room remains little changed since then and may be visited. After the Great War, a stained glass window by Gaudin was installed, depicting the historic meeting, also murals by Jonas depicting the French leaders pondering their dilemma at a crucial stage of the war.

The Gezaincourt Communal Cemetery Extension, on the south-west outskirts of the town, was one of the first to be designed by Lutyens; his mentor, Gertrude Jekyll, collaborated with him in the design of the planting and his assistant architect was Major Goldsmith. This cemetery probably provided the model for the many succeeding designs. Lutyens and Goldsmith were also responsible for Bagneux Military Cemetery, remotely situated at the end of the track leading from the rue de la Gare.

Doullens: Excursion

There are three pleasant outings from Doullens. The first is to the tiny township of **Lucheux**, 7 kms to the north-east, where the old town belfry forms a striking gateway

DOULLENS: Memorial to Foch

to a cobbled street of mainly eighteenth-century houses, rebuilt after fire-raising by Marlborough's troops in 1708. Standing above the main street is the medieval château where Joan of Arc was incarcerated on her way to Rouen. The town itself is small and old-fashioned, with some unusual rusticated lettering on the butcher's shop, and an extraordinary Art Nouveau villa suitably named 'Jalna'. The ogival vaulting of the choir of the church of St Léger is one of the earliest examples of the Gothic in northern France. The vigorously carved capitals however, dated 1140, representing the seven deadly sins, are full-bloodedly Romanesque.

The second excursion is to **Pas-en-Artois**, 7 kms to the east, a small town of great charm in a verdant valley. A plain eighteenth-century château is set in parkland which slopes down into the heart of the town, with its pretty church, and picturesque seventeenth- and eighteenth-

LUCHEUX: The town gateway and belfry

LUCHEUX: The Art Nouveau gateway of Jalna

century stone and brick houses. To the south, just off the D11, the charming château of **Raincheval** of 1719 may be visited. At the south end of the village of **Louvencourt**, 6 kms to the east, the British War Cemetery, designed by Blomfield, has an unusual feature in that the graves of the French soldiers have headstones modelled on the British pattern, instead of the customary concrete crosses, which was carried out at the request and subscription of the villagers.

The third excursion is westwards along the D938 – following the tranquil valley of the Authie. The pastoral landscape is dotted with covetable small châteaux. The late Laura Ashley used to live at Remaisnil and there is a particularly desirable example, Beauvoir-Rivière, at **Beauvoir-Wavans**. The small unspoilt town of **Auxi-le-Chateau**, on the frontier of Artois and Picardy, has a Flamboyant Gothic church – St Martin – noted for the remarkable carving of its vaulting. The church dominates a *quartier* of tightly packed old cottages. The Hôtel de Ville is neo-Gothic and there is a small museum devoted to local folklore. 5 kms to the south-west on the D941 at **Bernâtre**, old houses huddle picturesquely around the walls of an ancient château.

DUNKERQUE (Nord)

The northernmost town of France, swept with winds from the North Sea, and with a vast industrial sprawl, this major port, the third largest in France, much of it devoted to petro-chemicals and steel, is understandably off-putting to the average visitor. Yet Dunkerque has its attractions, despite substantial destruction in World War Two, and should not be too readily dismissed.

Dunkerque proper starts near the station and the Canal de Furnes. In the square Guynemer there survives, just, the Bains Dunkerquois, a ceramic and mosaic extravaganza in a Turkish style crossed with Art Nouveau. Two terracotta lions guard the entrance, but the building appears

93

neglected and in some danger. In the centre of the square is a striking red sandstone memorial by Desruelles, recording the valour of the sailors who fought on land during the First World War. A trumpeting lady angel exhorts a troop of marching sailors, and a horse-drawn gun carriage brings up the rear, all carved in a powerful relief style. In the town centre, the tall medieval belfry tower, with a war memorial by Frétel at its base, has a lift to the top, from where you can enjoy some marvellous views. Until 1940 it was manned as a look-out by generations of the Garcia family, father to son, over an astonishing period of six hundred years.

The fifteenth-century church of St Eloi, much restored and rebuilt, has a light and bright interior, almost square in plan. In a chapel on the south side is a Pietà by L. Piron, set above an altar with low-relief sculpture – unusual in that it is all of the 1930s.

In the main square the legendary sailor hero, Jean Bart, strikes a dashing pose in a good sculpture by David d'Angers. The Hôtel de Ville built between 1898 and 1901, is an early essay in the Flemish revival style by Cordonnier. Above the stairs a large stained glass window by Felix Gaudin (1898) shows, in a lively manner, Jean Bart's triumphant entry into the town after his victory over the Dutch at Texel in 1694. The facade carries a large sculpture by Edgar Boutry of Louis XIV, commemorating his purchase of the town from the English in 1662 – Cromwell having taken it four years earlier, when the Spanish were defeated at the battle of Dunkerque. Before then, the town had been a Spanish possession and selling it to the French was part of the deal that led ultimately to the marriage of Charles II to Catherine of Braganza. The statues on the facade are of local notables, sculpted by Augustin Peene.

The Musée des Beaux Arts, in a dull post-war building, has a good mix of sixteenth- and seventeenth-century Dutch and Flemish paintings and some more recent French art, including a big case of modern glass by Maurice Marinot. The large collection of ship models has an immediate appeal, and there is a gallery devoted to the Second World War. There is little else to see in the centre of the town, which was largely rebuilt in a dreary way after the destruction of 1940. Head instead towards the animation of the main port and shipyards particularly when the fishing fleet comes in – a scene that was painted by Signac in 1930. Cruises round the port are available in the summer. A museum is in preparation in the former tobacco warehouse on the quai de la Citadelle which will be devoted to the history and activities of the port. Now dominating the scene however, is an immense new Post-Modern building, the Communauté Urbaine, the administrative building of Dunkerque and its satellites.

To the east, beyond Edouard Lormier's victory column with its triumphant angel commemorating the Duke of York's unsuccessful siege of 1793, is the newly built and rather spectacular contemporary art museum, the Musée d'Art Contemporain, designed by Jean Willerval. It is set in a well landscaped park and surrounded by pools of water which effectively reflect the architecture; the harbour cranes provide a backcloth. Unfortunately the collection on display is not worth the effort, except for determined enthusiasts of such post-war art.

The eastern extension of Dunkerque is the resort suburb of **Malo-les-Bains**. On the sea front beyond the casino are some enjoyable turn of the century villas, such as 'Quo Vadis'; note also the 1920s house with penguin decorations. The whole area behind the seafront has a particularly *fin de siècle* flavour. Behind the casino is a strongly-sculpted monument of wounded and distressed soldiers.

Dunkirk – the English spelling of the town – strikes a strong chord in the minds of the English, but the tragic events of May-June 1940, when, despite the overwhelming weight of the German attacks, some 350,000 troops – the retreating British Expedi-

DUNKERQUE: The harbour　　　　　　　*GRAVELINES: 'La conversation'*

WORMHOUDT: Jeanne Devos museum

tionary Force and some 140,000 French soldiers – managed their epic escape to England thanks to the Royal Navy, RAF support and the famous flotilla of 'little ships', are rather weakly commemorated by an uninspiring memorial at the west end of the beach: a length of wall built with paving stones from the quays where the British troops embarked. Over 100,000 men were captured by the Germans. Dunkirk has become a legend of heroism which almost conceals the lamentable fact that we sent out an ill-prepared and ill-equipped force and almost lost our army at an early stage of the war. Dunkerque was the very last French town to be liberated, not until May 1945.

The Aquarian Museum in the avenue Faidherbe is another of the resort's diversions. For admirers of post-war architecture, the church of St Jean-Baptiste (1963), supposedly in the shape of a boat's prow, is worth a look for its successful interior with characteristic stained glass. The famous carnival, which originally launched the fishermen on their long, lonely and dangerous voyages to the north Atlantic, as far as Iceland, takes place on the weekend before Shrove Tuesday.

Also attached to Dunkerque, is the commune of **Rosendael** with its own important-looking Hôtel de Ville, in the customary Flemish style. Just to the east, the place de l'Abbé Bonpain is an enclave with a particular period flavour; the war memorial is a tall column crammed with active figures. On either side of the square are monuments by Ringot: to the cheery Abbé Bonpain, and a local worthy, Felix Coquelle. The pediment of the nearby 1930s building was presumably sculpted for a men's club – no ladies are present in the group of posers.

To the south on the route de Furnes, (the N1 towards Belgium), stands the British Memorial and cemetery. Although inaugurated in 1957 by the Queen, the building is characteristic of the 1920s War Graves Commission preferred style. The large etched glass window depicting the relief of Dunkirk is by the talented artist John Hutton – best known for his work at Coventry Cathedral.

Belfry and carillon enthusiasts should make a short excursion to **Cappelle-la-Grande**, on the southern outskirts of Dunkerque towards Bergues. A Post-Modern belfry, 40 metres high, built in 1985, continues this long Flemish tradition.

Dunkerque Excursion

To the west of the industrial sprawl of Dunkerque, is **Gravelines**, its character determined by Vauban's ramparts and the River Aa. This small town and port suffered badly from Panzer assaults during the defence of Dunkerque in 1940. There is a large main square dominated by the Hôtel de Ville of 1836 by Henry, cheerfully thronged on market day, with a belfry and a memorial to both World Wars consisting of two crouching soldiers below a column, on top of which is the French *coq*. On the outskirts of the town the windmill, built as recently as 1925, is the smallest in Flanders and was in use until 1966. The big plain brick church of St Willibrod has a good marble monument sculpted by Girardon, extensive panelling and a seventeenth-century organ. Attached to the church is a huge eighteenth-century stone cistern for storing water during a siege, with battered walls, an architectural term meaning that they incline, a characteristic of defensive buildings.

From the main square, a gateway leads into the Arsenal, now converted into a cultural centre. A museum of engravings, the Musée de la Gravure et de l'Estampe Originale, is housed in the former powderhouse of 1742, worth visiting for its architecture as well as the good temporary exhibitions; on the lawn is 'La Conversation', an eye-catching bronze group of well-endowed ladies by the sculptor Charles Gadenne (1977). The canal from Gravelines leads to **Petit-Fort-Phillipe**, at one time a haunt of English smugglers, now a small resort overshadowed by the presence of the

BERGUES: *The canal and town walls*

most powerful nuclear power station in the world, which produces ten per cent of the power needs of France. Off this coast, the Spanish Armada was defeated and dispersed by the English fleet in 1588.

From Gravelines turn south along the D11, then east via the D17 for about 18 kms across flat farmland with an intersecting network of drainage ditches, called *moëres* locally (pronounced 'moo-aah'), to reach the peaceful small town of **Bergues**. This Flemish wool town has something of the atmosphere of Bruges, and was well restored after damage in the First World War. The medieval centre is circular in plan and fringed by canals, which were important in the First World War for carrying supplies to the Front and bringing back the wounded. Now tranquil and little used, they provide good walks with tantalising glimpses through the gates which pierce the town walls. The main fortifications, by Vauban, are called the Couronne de Hondschoote. The heart of the town is almost overwhelmed by the monumental belfry, which is a tribute to the skill of the

bricklayer, as is the church of St Martin. Both these ancient buildings were destroyed in the Second World War and rebuilt by the architect Paul Gelis, but with simplified lines. The church contains post-war stained glass by Ingrand and Bertrand, and ceramic stations of the cross by Jeanne Champillon. The nearby shrapnel-scarred 1914–18 war memorial, by Ringot, depicts a sprawled, dying soldier.

The Musée Municipal should be visited for its good art collection (including the outstanding 'Le Joueur de Vielle' – the hurdy-gurdy player – by Georges de la Tour), housed in a seventeenth-century almshouse called the Mont-de-Piété. The gable end is a highly-accomplished piece of Baroque architectural scenery by Wenceslas Coebergher, a polymath who spent some years in Rome and Naples before returning to his native land full of ideas which included the introduction of almshouses to Flanders, and draining the Bergues marshes for cultivation.

There are agreeable walks in every direction. Creeper-clad houses of creamy yellow brick, often pilastered, are bright with window-boxes of geraniums in season. The Hôtel de Ville, with its blue marble ornamental detail, was rebuilt in 1872 by the architect Outters of Antwerp. A plaque and bust recall the poet Lamartine, who was a local *député*. The impressive vestiges of the ancient abbey of St Winoc, ruined at the Revolution, lie to the east, while Vauban's Cassel Gate, to the south, sports the sun emblem of Louis XIV in the pediment. In the leafy Place St Victor is one of the attractive cast-iron Wallace fountains donated by the English philanthropist, Sir Richard Wallace, best known for the famous collection in London named after him. Just outside the gates of the town, the early railway station of 1857 survives in good condition.

From Bergues go due east for 11 kms along the D110 to **Hondschoote**. An interesting way to appreciate this attractive Flemish town, with its main buildings ranged round a huge square, is by visiting the picturesque Hôtel de Ville. This is a typical gabled Flemish building of 1558, built of brick and stone, with an octagonal tower. It contains a small museum which includes a number of paintings. The best of these is a panoramic view of the Battle of Hondschoote of 1793, at which the French overcame the combined armies of Britain and Austria. Many features of the town are recognisable, including the famous windmill, which can be visited; now preserved, this wooden postmill is patently of the nineteenth century, but it contains a beam dated 1127, making it the oldest mill in Europe. Also featured in the painting is the church of St Vaast, an impressive building with a dramatic spire and some excellent eighteenth-century Baroque woodwork inside. There are other seventeenth- and eighteenth-century houses around the square, and a pretty cast-iron bandstand.

Next head south-westwards on the D55 via **Rexpoëde** and **West-Cappel** – both calm and pleasant villages with old churches – to the spruce main road village of **Wormhoudt**,

which boasts an Edwardian bandstand in the large central place. The handsome seventeenth-century tower, recently cleaned, of the church of St Winoc, closes the vista to the south. The essential visit in the village is to the secluded small Musée Jeanne Devos. Mlle. Devos, who died in 1989 at the age of 87, was a local professional photographer whose camera captured the essential flavour of Flanders from the early years of this century. She also sympathetically restored her pretty early eighteenth-century house and filled it with old Flemish furniture and objects. This is perhaps the easiest way to visit a private house of the region, with a traditional interior of great charm. Another local visit is to the eighteenth-century windmill on the Cassel road to the south.

On quite a different note, Wormhoudt is still remembered for the hideous massacre in 1940 of over eighty British soldiers, herded into a barn by the S.S. and then gunned down or blown up with hand grenades.

At Herzeele, 5 kms to the east, the characteristic creamy yellow brick of Flanders is still produced.

The D17 now leads westwards to **Esquelbec**, where the large central square is particularly pleasing. The attractive townscape is formed by a range of sixteenth- to nineteenth-century houses, many with decorative cast-iron balconies, a creeper-clad inn and the pink brick sixteenth-century *hallekerke* church of St Folquin – a type of church common in Flanders with three or five naves of equal height, and formerly used as the local market. Sensitively restored after a fire in 1976, the interior is decorated with modern art, which is not without merit. Behind the inn are views over a formal garden of trellised and espaliered parterres to the highly picturesque medieval château, framed by trees. This is in need of sympathetic restoration, as the famous 45-metre high hexagonal tower has recently collapsed, and the middle of the château has tumbled into the moat.

Leaving Esquelbec you cannot fail to see,

BERGUES: *The town centre*

ART DECO: *A typical 1920s doorway*

to the south, the town of **Cassel** on its hill top – a rarity in this flat part of Flanders, providing excellent views over the plain. It used to be said that five kingdoms could be seen from Cassel – France, England, Belgium, Holland and God's. The public garden at the top of the town has a wooden postmill and an equestrian statue of Marshal Foch by Georges Malissard – another cast of which can be found in Grosvenor Gardens in London. The largely triangular Grand'Place has a number of attractive old buildings. The gently Renaissance Hôtel de la Noble Cour or T'Landhuys houses a small museum; it is partly devoted to Foch, who made his headquarters here, there is a traditional Flemish kitchen, a local history collection and the handsomely panelled court room. Narrow cobbled streets fan out from the Grand'Place; both the Jesuit chapel, in a more sober Baroque than usual in the North, built of brick dressed with stone, and the Gothic church of Notre Dame, where Foch often came to pray, will be found close to the Porte de Dunkerque. Inside Notre Dame is a monument to Foch by Boutry, and a grand eighteenth-century organ, with the figures of King David and Ste Cecile marvellously silhouetted above. Now a restaurant with good views from its tables, the Hôtel de Schoebecque, in the rue du Maréchal Foch, housed the marshal and also received, at various times, George V, the King of Belgium, the Prince of Wales and Haig and Joffre. Sir William Orpen was in Cassel at the time as a war artist, as was Augustus John, and described the town with affection in his war reminiscences published in 1921; he was also one of the first to draw attention to the wretched life of the ordinary soldier during the war. It was at Cassel that the Grand Old Duke of York, of nursery rhyme fame, marched his 10,000 men up and down the hill in 1793; alas for them, it is very long and rather steep, and to make matters worse the English failed to take the town.

The giants Reuze Papa and Reuze Maman appear on Easter Monday. 7 kms to the west of Cassel is the old village of **Noordpeene**, the site of the battle in 1677, won by the French against a coalition of troops headed by William of Orange. It is worth visiting, since it seems to encapsulate the flavour of maritime Flanders.

HESDIN (Pas de Calais)

The principal focus of this very attractive small country town – created only in the sixteenth century, after the destruction in 1553 of Vieil-Hesdin, 6 kms away – is the main square – the place d'Armes. Large, cobbled and elegant, with a very agreeable French provincial atmosphere, its dominant feature is the Hôtel de Ville, a brick and stone building that was originally the palace of Marie of Hungary, the sister of Charles V and governor of the Low Countries. Its striking Renaissance porch of 1629, by Dom Dupont de Bruyas, was added when the palace became the Hôtel de Ville. Later extended, the building also acquired the tall belfry designed by Clovis Normand in 1876. The small museum with its tapestries can be visited on afternoons only.

The townscape will be familiar to those who remember the television series, 'Inspector Maigret', much of which was filmed in Hesdin.

Just off the square, the wealth of the town, which came partly from tapestry-making, is displayed by the splendid portal of the church of Notre Dame – an enjoyable profusion of notably secular late Renaissance detail, providing a welcome break from saints and effigies. The nearby rue des Nobles contains several handsome old town houses, including the quite grand Hotel Siougeat with a large forecourt. Behind the church, by the river Canche which flows through the town along an intimate route, is a bust of the Abbé Prevost, the author of *Manon Lescaut*, who was born here in 1697. Try the patisserie in the corner of the main square, which has excellent cakes, chocolate and local specialities, and other pleasant 1950s stained glass panels of baking and

HESDIN: *The church of Notre Dame*

HESDIN: *The Hôtel de Ville*

FAUQUEMBERGUES: *The war memorial*

other suitably sweet subjects. Those interested in such things should come to Hesdin on the first Sunday of each month for the regular crossbow tournaments which are a feature of the region.

Hesdin: South Excursion

Take the D928 south of Hesdin to the valley of the Authie, which follows a pleasant rural route to the sea below Berck. Quiet roads follow both banks, of which the northern is the prettier, winding through the woods and farms that fill the valley. This is a centre for basket-making, with workshops and shops at **Le Boisle**. The best architectural features of the area are the great classical gateways that mark the entry to the former abbey of **Dommartin**. It is not open to the public, but the rather English-looking park, the abbey ruins and the remains of the considerable dependencies can be easily seen from the road.

The D224 and then the D192 now follow the south bank of the Authie to **Argoules**, a small village of intimate charm with a sixteenth-century church, a manor house and old cottages around a green. The Gros Tilleul inn is an agreeable halt before visiting the huge Cistercian abbey of **Valloires**. This is of ancient foundation but was rebuilt on a grand scale in the eighteenth-century, after fire damage, to the designs of the architect Raoul Coigniart. His sober exterior conceals some very opulent interiors executed in 1750 by the sculptor Baron Pfaff de Pfaffenhoffen who had settled in Picardy after banishment from his native Austria following a duel. A spacious horseshoe-shaped entrance courtyard is enclosed by low outbuildings, including a dovecote of earlier date. The main building surrounds a large classical cloister with Doric arcading. In one corner a modest doorway leads into the astonishing abbey church. The tall white stone vaulted space provides an austere setting for Pfaffs's sumptuous carved work. A monumental carved oak organ fills the north wall and is adorned by swirling putti, musician-cherubs,

panels of musical instruments and powerful atlantes in the manner of Puget, crowned by the figure of King David. Two gilded angels hover giddily at roof level above the Rococo panelled choir stalls. The extraordinary ciborium, in the form of a palm tree, sprouting from the marble high altar, and the tall graceful choir screen are outstanding examples of eighteenth-century wrought-iron work, forged by J.B. Veyren of Corbie to designs of Michel-Ange Slodtz, who was known principally as a sculptor to Louis XV. Veyren's other major work is the choir-screen in Amiens Cathedral. The sacristy has the secular air of a drawing-room, with carved panelling by Pfaff and inset paintings by Parrocel.

The D192 continues westwards, past an odd nineteenth-century Gothic château standing above the river and a picturesque old water mill, to **Nampont St Martin**, straddling the N1. Just to the west of the village is a captivating small fortified château ringed by moats. It was rebuilt after its sacking by the troops of Phillip IV of Spain in 1635. It is highly photogenic but the owners are not very welcoming to photographers.

Hesdin: North Excursion

Head northwards from Hesdin along the D94 to **Auchy-lès-Hesdin**. Incongruously adjoining a huge textile mill, the abbey church of St Georges, where French knights were buried after Agincourt, has a curious facade, mixing Gothic, Classical and neo-Gothic features. The interior contains a putative Van Dyck. The D155 then leads northwards to **Fressin**, which has the ruins of a fifteenth-century château; despite restoration, the church should be visited for the Flamboyant Gothic reredos of the Crowning of the Virgin and the carvings of strange animals on the pillars. The village was the childhood home of the writer Bernanos, and provides the background for his famous interwar novels *Sous le Soleil de Satan* and *Journal d'un curé de campagne*. Both were made into excellent films shot on

AZINCOURT: A rural petrol station

VALLOIRES: Pfaffenhoffen's panelling

VALLOIRES: Interior of the chapel at the abbey

location in the area: the former by Pialat in 1987, the latter by Bresson in 1950.

Country lanes to the north-east lead to **Azincourt**, the scene of one of the bloodiest battles of the Hundred Years War, and known to the English for some reason – perhaps a mis-read manuscript – as Agincourt. Now a peaceful village, it has a small museum with a short audio-visual show describing the awesome battle of 1415, at which a whole generation of French nobility was wiped out on St Crispin's Day 1415, as so vividly depicted in Shakespeare's *Henry V*. After this, take refreshment in the nearby café. The traditional interior was installed by the present owner's grand-parents in the 1850s and, remarkably, survives almost unchanged. At the cross-roads, next to a charming little pantiled petrol station *à la* Lutyens, is a glass case containing an informative map of the battle lines. To the south there is another helpful description, a ceramic orientation table, at the junction of the D104 and the road to Maisoncelle.

In the nearby village of **Tramecourt**, where the Royal Flying Corps had an airfield, the family of one of the nobles killed at the Battle has inhabited the château since the eleventh century, though the building now appears to be mostly eighteenth-century. A strange 1920s monu-ment by Real del Sarte, at the end of the avenue, not at all characteristic of his work, has plaques which commemorate the deaths of three members of the family, deported by the Germans in 1945.

The surrounding fields in the village are unusually and attractively planted with tall trees set in from the enclosing hedgerows. To the north, the village church of **Verchin** has a very singular spire, twisted quite out of shape – the result of construction with unseasoned timbers. The 1608 *mise au tombeau*, or entombment, does not follow the usual dramatic treatment, but is sculpted in a touching, almost naive fashion.

To the north-west, the valley of the Aa provides a picturesque back-road route towards Calais. Starting at **Renty**, the road passes a pretty water mill, and outside the church the conventional war memorial is flanked by real artillery. At **Fauquembergues** the thirteenth-century church of St Léger has a handsome classical porch and overlooks a steeply sloping square with an excellent 1924 war memorial, with a bronze angel, by Léonce Alloy, a native of the town. Inside the church the stained glass by Laurant of Lambersart – near Lille – is of two periods, the 1930s and the 1950s. Tucked in a corner of the square, the 1898 war memorial has a striking figure of a soldier standing on a sort of grotto embedded with cannons and cannon balls.

At **Merck-St-Liévin**, the church of St Omer, standing proudly above the river, has several interesting features within, including an eighteenth-century pulpit.

LILLE (Nord)

The capital of the North, and flanked by the river Deûle, Lille is a vibrant, thrusting and prosperous provincial capital; it is the equivalent perhaps of Manchester – but unlike that once great mercantile city, the centre of which now seems a little deflated, Lille is renewing itself in a powerful way, without that shadowy feeling, so common in cities in the North of England, that former glory has been lost forever.

The citizens of Lille benefit from a number of practical post-war achievements, including a very stylish and efficient Metro, and a good motorway system, and an active and varied cultural life. The old centre is being sympathetically restored without the crushing hand of the highway engineer. There is a large university; a thriving orchestra; good ballet, opera and theatre; the largest bookshop in Europe, and one of the richest provincial fine arts museums in France. An important contemporary arts museum has been established within the conurbation, at the new town of Villeneuve d'Ascq. There are good road, rail and air links with the major centres of north-west

LILLE: La Voix du Nord building

Europe and the annual International Fair, on a permanent site, attracts nearly 500,000 visitors. During the first weekend of September the animation of the annual *braderie* takes over the whole city centre, with feasting on mussels and chips in the streets, street music, and an enormous flea-market.

Lille's first great period of expansion took place during the seventeenth century; initially a capital of the Spanish Low Countries, it became part of France in 1667, under Louis XIV. The King's engineer, Vauban – Sebastian Le Prestre, marquis de Vauban, constructed his masterpiece: a magnificent star-shaped Citadelle, which is still used by the army and is therefore not easily accessible, except by arrangements with the tourist office. The Germans executed many local resistance fighters here during World War I, and they are commemorated by a large monument 'A ses Fusillés' by Desruelles on the south side of the canal bridge which leads to the Citadelle – four defiant erect figures and one sprawled dead. Another monument is to be found on the north side of the same bridge: dedicated to the humble carrier pigeon – some 20,000 were used in the Great War – it is a large Art Deco composition in which the writhing serpent presumably signifies the evil enemy. By the bascule bridge to the east, two attenuated Art Deco ladies stand guard in memory of Achille Testelin. Nearby, the Jardin Vauban is a very agreeable small park, much needed in a city centre somewhat lacking in green spaces. At its west end, *fin de siècle* mansions look out over intricately-shaped espalier work created by the civic gardeners. Close by, at No 5 avenue de l'architecte Louis Cordonnier, are the former municiple baths, which have recently been restored. They were built in 1911 to the designs of Emile Dubuisson in a pretty Art Nouveau style with intricate woodwork and ceramic detail. To the south, in the square Rameau, the vaguely oriental Palais Rameau, built in 1878, has, at its south end, a large and handsome circular conservatory;

nearby, in the rue Patou, is a mansion with excellent ceramic portrait busts and details. To the south west of the Citadelle, in the boulevard de la Lorraine, a 1930s brewery, La Grande Brasserie, has a big Art Deco gateway.

The heart of the city is the Place Général de Gaulle, more commonly known as the Grand'Place, flanked by the long facade of the Vieille Bourse or stock exchange of 1652 – a big rectangle of Flemish Baroque by Desprez, built around a splendid courtyard. In the centre of the square is a column by Bra, commemorating local resistance in 1792 to the marauding Austrians; it is topped by a fierce goddess, modelled on the wife of the then mayor.

On the south side of the Place, the principal newspaper of Flanders, *La Voix du Nord* (renamed after the war owing to accusations of collaboration), is housed in an oversized stepped-gabled Flemish Art Deco pile of 1936, designed by Albert Laprade and built of gleaming white stone, with sculpted symbolic figures, by Raymond Couvègnes, climbing up its facade. Laprade was an interesting architect of the inter-war period; he designed one of the pavilions for the 1925 Paris Exposition des Arts Décoratifs, the 1931 Musée des Colonies at Paris, and a number of buildings for the 1937 Paris International Exhibition. Later, as an inspector of the Beaux Arts, he was influential in protecting historic town centres from redevelopment. However, one surprising lapse in his career can be observed in Lille, at the south end of the rue de Tournai, near the main station: a banal post-war tower-block, the Cité Administrative. Le Furet du Nord, on the west side of the Grand'Place, is reputedly the largest bookshop in Europe and adjoins FNAC, a large branch of the highly professional chain of shops specialising in music and photography. Mozart, as a child prodigy travelling through Europe, was lodged in one of the adjoining houses during an illness. It is now incorporated in the Grand Hôtel Bellevue, which retains some of its *fin de siècle* splendour.

To the south, in the rue Neuve, is a good old-fashioned bookshop, Emile Raoust & Cie. and around the corner, at No 7 rue du Sec Arembault, is the delightful Vidal umbrella shop, a completely intact *belle époque* establishment dating from 1884, retaining all its old fittings and ornate lamps.

To the west, in the place Rihours, the Gothic Palais Rihours of Philippe le Bon (now the tourist office) is flanked incongruously by a truly monumental war memorial, designed by Alleman and crowded with figures sculpted by Boutry.

Immediately east of the Grand'Place, the immense Nouvelle Bourse (1906–1920) imposes itself, with its very high belfry tower. It was designed by Louis Cordonnier in an urbane late-Renaissance style with stone predominant; its exuberance seems appropriate for the economical capital of the North. The adjoining Opéra is also by Cordonnier, but in an uncharacteristically classical style, with a vast sculpture high up, 'The Glorification of the Arts', which is a good set piece by H-J. Lefebvre, rather in the style of Carpeaux, but later in date and thus more fluid and less classical in execution. The side panels depict 'Tragedy', by Hector Lemaire, and 'Music' by A.A. Cordonnier. The Opéra was much appreciated by German officers during the 1914–18 War, when Lille was behind the German lines and occupied for almost the entire war. The handsome neo-Classical station, in view at the far end of the rue Faidherbe is actually the facade of the old Gare du Nord brought from Paris and re-erected here in 1865.

Just behind the Nouvelle Bourse, on the corner of the rue de la Clef, is a traditional café, the Café Carnot, with colourful tile panels inside. Around the corner, No 13 rue des Arts is of the Art Deco period, and at No 1 rue du Lombard, to the east, is the Hôtel Bide de Granville of 1773 where Lille's first cotton-spinning machine, imported from England at great risk, was installed in 1821. Opposite, the Musée Industriel & Commercial is housed in a 1628

building: the Hôtel du Lombard, designed by the polymath, Wenceslas Coebergher, but later ineptly restored.

South-east of the Grand'Place is the big church of St Maurice, which has the proportions of a cathedral; oddly enough, Lille does not have a traditional cathedral of its own. St Maurice was built over four centuries, but the result is surprisingly homogeneous: Gothic, with five naves of equal height, it is a typical Flemish *hallekerke*. On the south side of the church is an eighteenth-century bakery, with pretty blue tiles inside; the adjoining Maison du Renard dates from 1660. Glance opposite at an Art Nouveau-ish shop front.

The old town, *Vieux Lille*, stretches north of the Grand'Place. The seventeenth century produced a very particular and lively local Mannerist architecture of brick with vigorous stone details – quoins, pilasters, carved swags, garlands and masks – best seen in the rue de la Grande Chaussée, the place du Lion d'Or and the rue de la Monnaie. The most notable building in this street however, is the Hospice Comtesse, an ancient town building around a large courtyard, founded in 1237 by Jeanne de Constantinople, Comtesse de Flandre. Rebuilt in the fifteenth century it now houses a museum and should be visited for its late medieval interiors, which have a decided flavour of the Low Countries, and have been admirably preserved.

The large neo-Gothic church nearby, Notre Dame de la Treille, remains uncompleted, although building commenced in 1854. The English architects Clutton and Burges won the competition to build it but disappointingly their design was not executed (nor indeed was that of the winner of the second prize, G.E. Street, the architect of the Law Courts in the Strand).

In the rue Thiers, glance at a curious and erotic masonic panel: a nude woman bearing a torch and framed by sun-rays, standing over a rather masculine looking sphinx.

In the rue Esquermoise, the grand

LILLE: *The belfry of the Nouvelle Bourse and the Vieille Bourse (right foreground)*

LILLE: *The Hôtel de Ville*

teahouse, the Meert, should be visited for its old-fashioned atmosphere. Still with food in mind, L'Huitrière, nearby in the rue des Chats Bossus, is a justly celebrated Art Deco establishment, designed by Trannoy and Monoudoin in 1922. The restaurant upstairs is very good and not for the impecunious, but the delight of the place – the spacious shop on the ground floor, with its abundance of seafood – can be vicariously enjoyed. It has a complete and stimulating interior, with vivid blue and gold mosaic panels by Gentil & Bourdet, depicting fishy subjects.

Enjoyable Art Deco can also be found at the *boulangerie* in the rue Basse, with its geometric stained glass and bright swirly ceramics. On the eastern outskirts of the old town, the Porte de Gand and the Porte de Roubaix are massive 1621 Baroque gateways, defensive relics of the Spanish occupation. Further east, beyond the city motorway ring road, the Cimetière de l'Est is for morbid amateurs of *fin de siècle* sculpture. The suburb east of the cemetery contains an

impressive water-tower like a giant mushroom, and nearby, in the rue Fermat, a 1930s chapel by Levillain and Serex at a huge seminary, the chapelle du Grand Seminaire. To the north of *Vieux Ville*, the rue Royale was the aristocratic *quartier* of the eighteenth century. No 9 rue Princesse was the birthplace of Charles de Gaulle, and, its interior little changed, is now a small museum devoted to this illustrious Lillois. The town-house owned by the family of the writer Marguerite Yourcenar, is nearby at No 26 rue Jean Moulin.

At No 100 rue Royale, Monsieur Joly operates splendid old-fashioned banqueting rooms, with stained glass sky-lights, which give onto a large garden. At the south end of the street are the diluted Art Nouveau flower shop, 'Au Cyclamen'; a 1930s dairy, 'Au Moulin de Cassel'; and, adjoining it, an old-fashioned bookshop, the librairie Réné Giard, founded in 1854. South-west of the Grand'Place, the rue Nationale passes the leafy square Jussieu; a sentimental sculpture by Deplechin of a young lace-maker singing

LILLE: The Opéra

LILLE: The chapel of the Réduit

a lullaby to her baby, seated below a 1902 Art Nouveau column with a bust of Desrousseaux, commemorates a composer of traditional songs dear to the Lillois. Just around the corner, at No 2 rue du Vert Bois is the 1910 house of the architect, Horace Pouillet, with good Art Nouveau wrought-iron balconies. Also to be found in the square, to the north, is another huge monument designed by Allcman, with an equestrian statue of Marshal Foch sculpted by Boutry.

Turn down the main axis of the city, the boulevard de la Liberté, to the spacious place de la République with its impressive metro station successfully incorporated. A very good bronze equestrian statue of General Faidherbe by Antonin Mercié (1896) looks across to the ponderous Second Empire bulks of the Préfecture and the Musée des Beaux Arts at each end of the Place. The latter is one of the richest fine art museums in provincial France and an essential visit. It is renowned for its Goyas, but the collection ranges widely, from Donatello to the Impressionists. Due south of the museum, the nineteenth-century church of St Michel in the place Philippe le Bon is dull, but provides a distinctive landmark in this Faculty *quartier*. The expressive monument to Pasteur of innoculation fame (who carried out much research in Lille), was designed by Louis Cordonnier and sculpted by A.A. Cordonnier (1897); the lady holding her child is particularly touching.

Turn the corner by the church into the rue de Fleurus for the astonishing and eccentric Maison Coilliot at No 14, a high point of European Art Nouveau architecture. Designed in 1898 by Hector Guimard, of Paris Metro fame, for a ceramic merchant (and still owned by the family), it demonstrates an ingenious means of turning a narrow terrace house into something quite spectacular. Supposedly inspired by a Gustave Doré drawing, Guimard set an open first floor loggia at an angle to the street, framed by inwardly curving arches. The patented hard-wearing ceramic (*lave émaillé*) for the facade was provided by Gillet of Paris. The colour subtly softens from dark at the base to pale above to create vertical emphasis. However, the style did not catch on in the region – it was too *avant garde* for the conservative Lillois, who had mostly, in any case, erected their mansions during the prosperous earlier decades.

Just to the east, the place Jeanne d'Arc has a standard statue of the heroine. Towards the south end of the boulevard de la Liberté are the *fin de siècle* Bains Lillois, by Albert Baert (1892) with ceramic decoration. Further east, the *Quartier* St Sauveur was once a working-class area of legendary misery, but has been mostly rebuilt. To the

LILLE: *Guimard's Maison Coilliot*

south, the 1682 Porte de Paris, by Simon Vollant, in the middle of a huge roundabout, is the mighty late Baroque triumphal arch in honour of Louis XIV; on its north elevation it looks more like a large pavilion.

The belfry of Emile Dubuisson's Hôtel de Ville nearby, of 1930, soars to 104 metres. A Flemish version of the Art Deco style, its slim silhouette demonstrates the power of reinforced concrete to create a remarkably tall structure on a very narrow base. At the base, sculpted by Charles Sarrabezolles, are the attenuated figures of the giants Lyderic and Phinaert, the founders of the city according to legend. The belfry can be visited for views over the city. In the nearby rue du Réduit, the pretty Louis XV stone Chapelle du Réduit stands in a leafy courtyard flanked by brick houses of the same date. Further along the street, the massive fifteenth-century stone Noble Tour is now a memorial to the Resistance, with sculpture by Andre Bizet-Lindet (his work for the 1937 Musée d'Art Moderne in Paris was excellent but here, as so often with post-war Resistance memorials, the art is not up to much). In the rue St Sauveur, the Pavillon St Saveur is an attractive but lonely survivor of an eighteenth-century cloister.

The attractions to the south-west area of the city are more dispersed. In the place Sebastopol, opposite the theatre, the restaurant Chez Etienne has a 1930s facade and ambience; to the north, the main market, the Halles Centrales, is the usual big cast-iron framed nineteenth-century structure. Opposite, the Rendezvous des Bouchers is a typical old café; and around the corner, at No 30 rue Massena, is an old family butcher's shop with a tiled interior of the early 1900s. The adjoining grocer's shop has old gilt lettered signs. Further south-west is the ethnically mixed *quartier* known as Wazemmes. There is a busy and colourful fruit and vegetable market here on Sunday mornings in the place Nouvelle Aventure; next to the church of St Pierre and St Paul is a section devoted to bric-à-brac. On the south side of the Place, a *charcuterie* sports 1930s stained glass of cheerful pigs, clearly oblivious of their fate.

Excursion to the Environs of Lille to the West & North

Devotees of late nineteenth-century eclectic villa architecture should cruise around the prosperous suburb of **Lambersart**, just north of the Citadelle, an area which has very much the feel of · Brussels, particularly in the avenue Foch, the avenue de l'Amiral Courbet and the avenue de l'Hippodrome, where there are some *fin de siècle* eccentricities. Architecture of a more urban type will be found in the adjoining suburb of **La Madeleine** to the east. Its Hôtel de Ville is by Cordonnier, of 1865; later, in 1888, he designed the adjoining church of Ste Marie-Madeleine, in a so-called Byzantine style. Both are less than his best. Tucked away off the avenue Simone, Notre Dame de Lourdes by Levillain and Serex is a large brick church adorned with sculpture panels, built in 1935 in a style which is not easy to classify, neither moderne nor Art Deco.

To the north is **Marquette-lez-Lille**, where the only item of interest is Les Grands Moulins of 1934, incongruously using the domestic Flemish elements of dormers and stepped gables to adorn an immense industrial building. Further north is **Wambrechies** a small canal-port town, which has its own sense of place, distinct from the suburbs. The big church is ugly, but gives character to the townscape. The nearby *pharmacie* has its original fittings; the Hôtel de Ville of 1868 by the prolific local architect Maillard is one of the earliest examples of Flemish revivalism, with strikingly patterned diaper brickwork. By the banks of the canal is the dour seventeenth-century Château Robersart; next to the canal bridge, the Claeyssens distillery still produces, by traditional methods, the famous gin called *genièvre*. On the northern edge of the town, the Ancienne Filature is a handsome 1926 Art Deco industrial building by Granet, with a tall brick central tower and a long fully glazed facade.

Now take the D308 northwards across gently undulating farmland towards the Belgian border and the small ribbon-making town of **Comines**; astride the river Lys, one half is in Belgium, and the other in France. This ancient township was virtually wiped out in the 1914–18 War. Out of the ashes, two really good buildings emerged, which stand opposite each other in the main square. Louis Cordonnier produced one of his inevitable neo-Flemish Hôtel de Ville, but this one is wonderfully eccentric. The belfry, with its bulbous tower, supposedly echoes the silhouette of its predecessor. Inside, stained glass above the main staircase illustrates a glorious past; the massive beams are now carried out in concrete.

The mayor of the day wanted a unique new church and the result, the church of St Chrysole, is an extraordinary neo-Byzantine building, conceived by Maurice Storez, an architect from Normandy, but inspired by the work of the remarkable architect-monk, Dom Paul Bellot. Both men were members of l'Arche, a Catholic association devoted to promoting sacred art. Financial constraints enforced the use of concrete framing for the structure, and the result is strikingly successful, Storez, having carefully studied the latest techniques of reinforced concrete, employed them with skill to produce his desired result. The plan is a Greek cross with a vast octagonal crossing. Exposed concrete ribs soar up to support the central cupola. The interior is bathed in a mysterious light created by the vividly-coloured stained glass designed by Hollart. When Storez was eventually forced to give up the project, Dom Bellot took over, and created a marvellous Expressionist interior with the collaboration of a number of artist-craftsmen, both local and from Paris, including Gaudin for the mosaics and Fillon for the communion rails. The walls are highly patterned with decorative brickwork and vitrified brick motifs in a vigorous polychromy. The wrought-iron grilles, gates and light fittings, and Hollart's expressive stations of the cross, all add to the completeness of this extraordinary building of the 1920s and 1930s. Outside, at the foot of the very tall belfry tower – not completed until 1937, is the war memorial of 1929, designed by Cordonnier and sculpted by Masselot.

Now head south-east to **Bondues**. The roadside memorial to the sixty-eight 'Fusillés du Fort de Bondues' is a tall pylon with the Cross of Lorraine and the usual Resistance motif of a manacled man. To the east is a well kept château – Le Vert Bois of 1743 – which is an oasis in an area that is either industrial or suburban-rural. It is well worth the detour. In its verdant setting, which effectively keeps the rather featureless landscape of the area at bay, it makes a pretty eighteenth-century scene, an elegant classical building surrounded by a moat, flanked by two little pavilions and approached through the archway of a stable block of earlier date complete with

dovecote. The interior is richly furnished, giving the lie to a common English belief that all French château are empty and dusty. Apart from clearly enjoying his château, the owner, Monsieur Prouvost, also collects Impressionist paintings. His interests in these and later works of art have led him to establish a foundation for contemporary art, Le Septentrion (which means pertaining to the north), pleasantly housed in the specially converted barn buildings nearby, in which art exhibitions are regularly held.

Now head eastwards across the A1 Motorway into the prosperous Tourcoing suburb of **Mouvaux**. At No 202 boulevard de la Marne, and easily appreciated from the road, is a 1930s recreation of a Normandy manor house, *rus in urbe*, a highly picturesque and mellow house which continues the Arts and Crafts tradition and is in striking contrast to the *moderne* Villa Cavroix of the same date (see the entry for Croix).

Lille Excursion: Tourcoing and Roubaix

Still important textile centres, these towns, together with Lille, form a vast urban agglomeration, a sort of European Los Angeles. **Tourcoing** is the less interesting of the two, but it has some redeeming features, notably the splendid neo-Baroque Hôtel de Ville of 1885, clearly inspired by the New Louvre, designed by the prominent local architect Charles Maillard, in the place de la République, and the very dramatic war memorial in the rue Faidherbe – a powerful creation related in style to that at Cambrai, but even more dynamic. The Hôtel de Ville contains a huge, and suitably heroic, painting by Bouttigny of the battle of Tourcoing (1794), at which the French defeated the Anglo-Austrian armies, and in the same room there are lively murals painted by Jugran in 1909, showing the locals *en fête*.

Close by, the Musée des Beaux Arts is housed in a mansion in which the composer Albert Roussel lived as a child. For a

ROUBAIX: *The Roubaix-Lille tramway*

ROUBAIX: *The Resistance memorial*

prosperous town, the collection is rather disappointing. A striking *belle époque* painting by Clairin shows the actress Sarah Bernhardt lying provocatively on a tiger skin, while above the staircase is a vast *pointilliste* canvas by Henri Martin. The picturesque house opposite the museum was built in 1910, as the home of a collector of antiquities. The tall spire visible to the south is the belfry of the Chamber of Commerce – built in 1906, in what was clearly a period of commercial prosperity. To the west, in the rue Nationale, after a sign proclaiming 'Rochdale 650 kms', the church of Notre Dame des Anges by Maillard is remarkable for its vast Second Empire interior; unusually for that period, it is not Gothic, but neo-Classical in style. In the parallel street, rue de Lille, the former Hôtel Malard of 1883, at No 100, now a cultural centre, retains much of its eclectic interior decoration, including tapestries, plasterwork

and fireplaces. The Art Nouveau chimney-piece in a front room upstairs is particularly pretty.

Any visit to **Roubaix** should really start at the station, a striking and original design by Dunnett of 1888, with a tall glazed facade flanked by pavilions. From here a wide boulevard, the avenue J. Lebas, leads towards the Grand'Place – passing an erotic Resistance monument by Lemaire, of a manacled nude woman, and a charming old fashioned hat shop, the Chapellerie des Beaux Arts. The lively Grand'Place was familiar to Gauguin, who was employed in Roubaix for a while. Here the medieval but much rebuilt church of St Martin faces the huge and proud Hôtel de Ville of 1911, the work of Victor Laloux, the architect of the Gare d'Orsay – now the Musée d'Orsay – in Paris. It has good sculpted allegorical panels of local industries by a number of talented local sculptors: A.A. Cordonnier, Edgar

Boutry, Léon Fagel, André Laoust, Corneille Theunissen and Hippolyte-Jules Lefebvre. The interior has a monumental staircase and a wall painting by René Cogghe, which depicts the granting of the medieval town charter. To the south, in the boulevard Maréchal Leclerc, is a monument to J. Lebas, by a local sculptor, Alfred Jaeger, still in an Art Deco style despite being post-war. A deputy mayor who died after being deported by the Nazis, Lebas was a popular local figure who espoused the causes of paid holidays for the workers and a forty-hour week. To the west is the chunky war memorial, a characteristic work of Alexandre Descatoire, with a powerful woman clutching a cornucopia astride a serpent. Nearby, at No 16, is the 1904 house of the architect Emile Dervaux. Its Art Nouveau style is related to contemporary work emanating from Nancy, in eastern France, rather than the local influence of Guimard. Close by, just to the west, the huge crenellated factory, modelled on Manningham Mills at Bradford, is now being converted to house the Archives du Monde de Travail.

The boulevard Maréchal Leclerc continues into the boulevard du General de Gaulle, a leafy avenue which shades the tramline which runs down its centre, and leads to the beautifully kept Parc Barbieux, which is dotted with sculpture. As so often in France resist the temptation to picnic or even sit on the immaculate lawns; you will be chased off to a bench.

Tourcoing – Roubaix: Excursion

Just south of the Parc Barbieux is the leafy suburb of **Croix**. Take the rue d'Hem and soon on the left is the rue J.F. Kennedy where, at No 60, disciples of the International Modern Movement will be disappointed to find that the enormous Villa Cavroix of 1932, by one of the gods, the Paris architect, Robert Mallet-Stevens, best known for his white Cubist villas, is in a forlorn state. The brick cladding on the

HEM: Interior of the chapel of Ste Thérèse

streamlined facade is dropping off, revealing the concrete frame, and the swimming pool is empty. Those traditionalists who enjoyed the house at Mouvaux, of the same date, perhaps uncharitably will crow.

Now continue southwards to **Hem**, an outlying suburb of Roubaix. In the rue de Croix is the chapel of Ste Thérèse, designed by the Swiss architect Hermann Baur in 1958. If this excellent example of contemporary architecture were better known, modern enthusiasts would make a pilgrimage to it in large numbers. Screened behind a hedge, a path leads past a picturesque group of old pantiled and white-painted cottages and a detached bell tower. The chapel is particularly redolent of the era of late Corbusier and Picasso. A wall of abstract stained glass, by Alfred Manessier, gives a soft light to the interior; it takes a few minutes for the eyes to become accustomed to the light and to appreciate the admirable and elegantly fitted interior

BOUVINES: Stained glass in the church of St Pierre

with its sculpture, mosaics, furniture and a tapestry after Rouault.

Continue on to the showpiece new town of **Villeneuve d'Ascq**; it is confusingly laid out, like Milton Keynes, and just as easy to get lost in. Unlike the latter, it has an outstanding new modern art museum, the Musée d'Art Moderne du Nord, set in a pleasant park dotted with sculpture, and the collection includes works by such artists as Picasso, Braque, Leger, Klee and Miro. The new town has re-erected several old windmills nearby, rather incongruously plonked together, far from their natural setting.

Assuming you can find your way out of Villeneuve, continue south for a few kms along the D955 to **Bouvines**. Here, surrounded by suburbia, is a rather dreary looking church. Modelled, in a very general sense, on Sainte-Chapelle in Paris, the church of St Pierre is remarkable in that it was specially built, in 1887, as the setting for a striking group of twenty one stained glass windows, designed by Lucien Magne and executed by the Champigneulles brothers of Bar-le-Duc. The sequence tells the story of the great battle of July 1214, at which the French king, Philippe-Auguste, defeated the allied armies of King John of England, the Emperor Otto of Germany and the Counts of Boulogne, Hainault and Flanders. Its rich colours and lively compositions make this a very rewarding detour. Less exciting, however, is a wander through the backstreets of **Cysoing**, just to the south, in search of the elegant obelisk raised by the local *abbé* in 1750 to commemorate the visit of Louis XV in May 1744.

Now take the D43 westwards to **Seclin**, passing en route a 1932 post office at **Fretin**, with a wonderful green tiled facade. Seclin has an imposing but rather dull thirteenth-century church; much more enjoyable is the seventeenth-century Flemish Baroque Vieil Hôpital, with a long facade of pink brick with stone dressings, set behind generous lawns. The heart of the building is a peaceful Doric arcaded cloister around a large cobbled courtyard. On the east side, of earlier date, is the stepped-gabled facade of the salle des malades – where the nuns received the sick – and the chapel.

To the north is **Loos**, notable mainly for its Hôtel de Ville of 1884, an early work of the neo-Flemish revival, and for once completely symmetrical, with its tall belfry tower rising in the centre. It was designed by Louis Cordonnier in the same year that he won a competition prize for the Bourse in Amsterdam.

The celebrated gin distillery – Les Genièvres de Loos – may be visited. It is one of only three establishments still producing this speciality of the North. The Tourcoing/Roubaix region is noted for the game of *bourle*, a sort of bowls played with flat wooden discs, the centre for which is **Wattrelos**. Be warned: games can last for hours.

MAUBEUGE (Nord)

Largely destroyed during a bombing raid in 1940, Maubeuge is an unprepossessing town. Its centre, designed by André Lurçat, is 1950s austerity at its worse, a featureless style that has not improved with the passage of time. Lurçat's church of St Pierre & St Paul is slightly better, and its mosaics – designed by André's brother Jean, and made at Murano – may appeal to lovers of the 1950s. Apart from the new buildings there is a good range of Vauban fortifications, including a handsome 1685 barracks block that incorporates the old town gate, the Porte de Mons; a seventeenth-century Jesuit Baroque college; and a fine bronze monument of 1895 – a lively work by Léon Fagel – commemorating the battle of Wattignies (1793). The Musée Henri Boez, housed in an eighteenth-century building in the rue du Chapitre, is one of the cultural attractions of the town, with its modest but pleasing collection of paintings and ceramics.

Although Maubeuge was the birthplace of the celebrated painter Jean Gossart, also known as Mabuse (1478–1533), in more recent times the town has been better known for armaments and metal industries. This probably explains why an old tank of about 1940 is parked in the main square. Those who are determined to visit Maubeuge should come in July during the beer festival, or at Easter when there is a Mabuse folk festival.

Maubeuge: Excursion

About 14 kms to the west along the N49 is **Bavay**, a little town known for its Roman remains and for a local sweet known as a *chique*. Some seventeenth- and eighteenth-century buildings overlook the main square, but the ruins of Roman Bagacum are its best feature. Most can be seen adequately from a car, but for those interested in archaeology there is a good museum. North of Bavay, in an area of marble quarries, is **Bellignies**, where there is a museum of marble.

Malplaquet, the site of Marlborough's great victory of 1709, lies to the north-east. The museum, Le Musée de Malplaquet, evokes the battle, in which 32,000 men were killed and 22,000 wounded. Of more recent interest is **Boussois**, 6 kms east of Maubeuge, where the church of St Martin was built in 1928, of glass bricks from a local factory.

ROYE (Somme)

There can be no better example of the shortcomings of the standard guides than Roye. Short entries dismiss the town as being largely industrial and rebuilt after the 1914–18 war – including the church which did, however, retain its sixteenth-century choir. In fact the only thing in Roye that is definitely not worth the detour is this sixteenth-century choir, which is completely overshadowed by, and inconsequentially attached to, one of the major Art Deco churches of northern France – the church of St Pierre. Even if you are unsympathetic to the twentieth-century, this should not be missed – in fact, it would be hard to do so, since the powerful and thrusting concrete and brick 70-metre tower dominates the town, inviting closer inspection. Designed by Duval and Gonse – the Parisian architects responsible for a number of modernist buildings in the region – and completed in 1932, with the collaboration of the sculptor, Raymond Couvègnes, this church is a fitting memorial to its period, and to the post-war reconstruction of northern France. The architects must have been inspired by the 1922 church at Le Raincy near Paris, Perret's seminal work.

Above the main door is a good low-relief sculptured panel, while further panels decorate the porch. However, it is the interior which provides a particularly dynamic expression of the Art Deco style. The building has a remarkable unity, but its special features are the excellent murals by Henri Marret, and two sequences of stained glass, one dating from 1937, the other probably earlier, the very Paris 1925-style metalwork; and restrained modernist pulpit and confessionals, the font, looks like a smart piece of 1930s table silver, the low-relief carved stations of the cross; and – especially exciting – the splendid ceramic-tiled side altars, with sculpted figures, angels, decorative lettering and altar rails, all in a wonderful range of vivid colours. The *mise au tombeau* is in traditional form, but the figures are in ceramic, boldly coloured. Be sure not to miss the recumbent figure of a soldier in one of the side chapels.

Roye also has an Art Deco Hôtel de Ville in the main square – it is late and rather lumpy, but the tall clock tower is distinctive. The interior is plain except for the cheerful stained glass panel, lighting the staircase, of *le coq gaulois*, the cockerel being the emblem of the Frenchman's fighting spirit.

The Péronne road (N17) from the centre passes the public tennis courts, with crossed rackets elegantly carved in stone on the gate piers, and further along on the left is a relic of Roye's importance as a busy staging post on the Lyon-Boulogne route: the former Relais de Postes, now a farmyard, with splendid arcaded ranges of stables with stone columns.

Roye: Excursion

Take the N17 southwards for 6 kms and turn right to **Tilloloy**, for the château, a particularly handsome brick and stone structure set in a huge park, apparently Louis XIV, but actually a post-1914 reconstruction of the seventeenty-century original, and a marvellous replica.

The church of Notre Dame de Lorette, of 1530, has a Renaissance portal and good tombs inside, with sculptures of kneeling figures. Continuing westwards, the huge, mostly open landscape of farmland is on a grand scale, broken only occasionally by belts of woodland and copses. There are plenty of farming villages, but they look remarkably similar, and are generally rather unexciting. The river valleys which cut through the plains are quite attractive, especially those of the Selle, Noye, and Brache. **Montdidier**, however, has an appeal all of its own, partly because of its siting on a slope, and partly because of its remarkable unity of style, having been entirely rebuilt in the 1920s after its destruction in the First World War. It is a town in which to spend a little time: discovering the small-scale pleasures of its architecture, and its variety of 1920s details. The best building is without doubt the Hôtel de Ville (1925) by Duval and Gonse. This is confident civic Art Deco with sculpted panels by Raymond Couvègnes, best known for his work for the Paris 1937 International Exhibition, metal-work and other features. The church, by contrast, is very poor – a large pile of tired Gothic. Those in search of the unusual might enjoy the statue of Antoine Parmentier, a locally born chemist who promoted the potato as a source of healthy food. He died in 1813, but his name lives on today, in the form of the popular dish, *hachis Parmentier* (shepherd's pie to the English).

A detour of 15 kms to the north, leads to the village of **Arvillers**, where the porch of the church of St Martin displays a very strong 1920s sculpture of the crucifixion curiously supported by massive Greek Doric columns. The sculpture is unsigned but is probably by Couvègnes and the whole design by Duval and Gonse.

The D26 westwards from Montdidier, over rolling countryside, passes a rather striking 1920s farm and stud and two good memorials near **Cantigny**, commemorating the American 1st Division, which captured the village on 28 May 1918 – its first engagement. Both feature eagles, but in radically different ways. Continue west for the high points of the area at **Folleville**: there is a ruined fifteenth-century château here, but one must concentrate on the church of St Jacques-le-Majeur of 1524, the interior of which is worth a pilgrimage. The rich Flamboyant Gothic choir is made out-standing by the tombs of the Lannoy family. The first, with its recumbent effigies of Raoul de Lannoy and his wife Jeanne, carved

FOLLEVILLE: Interior of the church

MONTDIDIER: Monument to Parmentier

MOREUIL: The church porch

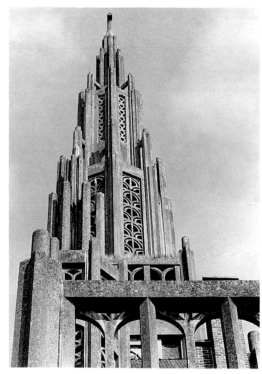

MOREUIL: The 1928 church tower

117

in Genoa in 1507 by Antonio della Porta and Pacce Gaggini, is an extravagant and delightful riot of Renaissance details, though framed in a Gothic sepulchre. Nearby executed some fifty years later, is the tomb of François de Lannoy, son of Raoul, and his wife Marie, demonstrating the later transitional style of sculpture. Work of this quality is rare in the North of France, and that at Folleville is exceptional by any standards. There are also some decent pews and a fine wooden pulpit in a rustic Baroque, from which St Vincent de Paul first preached in January 1617.

Opposite the church is some light relief in the form of a kind of garden shed: the very modest village hall of Folleville.

Northwards the D14 leads to **Moreuil**. As you approach this little market town, you cannot fail to notice the tall pierced concrete tower of the church of St Vaast. This splendid 1928 *moderne* church – with a rich array of low-relief carving by Raymond Couvègnes – is clearly another work by the talented team of Duval and Gonse. In this case the tower and the facade are attached to an earlier building of little interest. The porch is a very successful Art Deco composition with characteristic lamp standards. Nearby is the Hôtel de Ville, also of the 1920s, but not very exciting. Rather better is the war memorial in the market square opposite, commemorating the Franco-Prussian conflict as well as the First World War, with its lively and larger than life figure of a soldier by Albert Roze.

MOREUIL: *The war memorial*

Leaving Moreuil northwards by the D23 one comes to another memorial, an obelisk with a very striking and dynamic 1920s panel, commemorating the spot where the French 31st Army Corps broke the German lines on 8 August 1918, effectively marking the beginning of the end of the First World War. The Germans knocked it down in 1940, but it was rescued and resurrected after the war.

ST OMER (Pas de Calais)

St Omer, the capital of the Audomarois region of Artois close to the Flemish border, is a proper old-fashioned town with an elegant air, thanks to its aristocratic past and an absence of heavy industry – having refused to welcome the early development of the railways. It gives the impression of having escaped the damage of both World Wars, although this is not in fact strictly true.

It is the closest town to England to have that very particular character which endears France to the English. The English who passed through earlier, such as Nelson, who lodged here with an English parson in 1783 and entertained thoughts of marrying one of his daughters, or Marlborough, or more recently, the Royal Flying Corps, have left no traces, though at No 50 rue Carnot, there is a blue plaque, similar to those in London, which recalls the death of Field Marshal Lord Roberts of pneumonia in 1914. The attractions of this old wool town reveal themselves in an undramatic way. The close-knit cobbled streets are lined with handsome seventeenth- and eigheenth-century houses, often with giant pilasters – a local feature – and there are occasional Art Nouveau and Art Deco flourishes. The remains of Vauban's ramparts have been transformed into a dramatic terrace, which forms the principal feature of the beautiful *Jardin Public*, with its characteristic band-stand and sculpture, including the Duc d'Orleans by Raggi (1844).

Opposite the park, the church of Notre Dame is discreetly tucked into a corner of the town; yet this majestic church, built between the thirteenth and the fifteenth centuries, is immense – 100 metres long – and full of riches. An astonishing Baroque organ fills the west end in an extravagant way, topped by King David and St Cecilia, the patron saint of music. A Rubens Descent from the Cross is hung in a corner above the fifteenth-century inscribed slabs which pave the floor. The side chapels have rich polychrome marble screens, and there are striking tombs of Saint Omer, of the thirteenth century, and Eustache de Croÿ, the Bishop of Arras, kneeling above Christ recumbent, dating from the sixteenth century. Sculpted alabasters include a charming depiction of the Madonna with a cat. Next to the north door, through which the victorious Louis XIV entered in 1677, there is a powerful thirteenth-century sculpture of the Grand Dieu; and above it is a 1558 astronomical clock. Opposite the north door, by contrast, are Art Deco railings around a First World War Memorial. Above the south door, on the outside, there is a fourteenth-century Virgin and a Last Judgement.

After leaving Notre Dame, walk down to the place Sithieu, where the apparently eighteenth-century statue of the composer Monsigny is actually of 1905. To the east the Baroque Jesuit chapel of 1639 soars dramatically above the surrounding houses. Nearby is a Bibliothèque, containing carved panelling and a valuable collection of books and manuscripts, while opposite is the Dutch-gabled seminary. In the rue St Bertin, the pilastered College of Jesuits, where Daniel O'Connell was a pupil, has a plaque describing its varied history since its foundation in 1592 by English Jesuits who later moved on to found the public school of Stonyhurst. The street leads to the romantic Gothic ruins of the abbey of St Bertin, which should ideally be seen in moonlight. In front of it is a statue of Abbé Suger, the counsellor of two kings of France, and for whom the Gothic style was effectively created with the construction of the choir of St Denis near Paris (1140–44), a building which revolutionized architecture. Nearby an ornately carved door from the Brasserie Dumont adorns a private house. Towards the station, the curious 1914–18 war memorial is of an ample lady holding a dove and standing on a crocodile – the symbolism of the latter is unclear.

Beyond looms the palatial station of 1903 on the far side of the river Aa, which is here a canal, with quays and warehouses stretching to the west.

Heading back towards the centre of the town, the Hôtel Sandelin is an essential visit: this elegant stone mansion of 1777 built for the Vicomtesse de Fruges as a town house for diversion from winters in the country, is an excellent museum of fine and decorative arts, the Musée de l'Hôtel Sandelin. Gates in the Louis Quinze style, though made in 1926, form the entrance to a large cobbled forecourt which leads to a spacious entrance hall, where a serpentine Rococo staircase is dominated by a vast late nineteenth-century erotic canvas inspired by Rubens, 'Les Sirènes', by a local painter, Léon Belly. An *enfilade* of handsomely panelled rooms overlooks the garden. There is good Louis XV furniture, and a number of worthwhile pictures by Boilly, Greuze and Lepicié, as well as by Dutch and Flemish artists. The outstanding treasure is the celebrated base of the Cross of St Bertin, with its gold and enamel twelfth-century craftsmanship. Other rooms contain a profusion of clay pipes, a reminder of the former local tobacco industry, some engaging models showing the history of the town and a good many old weapons Upstairs is a large ceramic collection, which includes the unusual deep blue St Omer ware and an oddment: a Rococo ceramic chimneypiece from Bruges.

A few steps to the west, the place Victor Hugo has the splendid 1757 fountain of Ste Aldegonde tacked onto an eighteenth-century facade. It is a pity that the current

ST OMER: The church of Notre Dame

ST OMER: Fountain in the Place Victor Hugo

ARQUES: The Fontinettes Boat-Lift

owners, a bank, have defaced the facade with their vulgar lettering. Also in the square is a shopfront which, though carved with classical motifs, is difficult to date. Off to the south, in the rue des Tribunaux, a gigantic portal conceals the splendid former bishop's palace (1680–1701) designed by Jules Hardouin Mansart, now the Palais de Justice. To the west of the Place Victor Hugo, the eighteenth-century house of Monsieur Henri Dupuis, in the street of the same name, is now the eccentric Musée Henri Dupuis, which contains his manic collection of 25,000 shells and 2500 stuffed birds; more endearing perhaps is the old Flemish kitchen, a far cry from the age of formica with its huge fireplace lined with pretty blue Dutch tiles, and the traditional calm of Dupuis' study, with a bust of him by Louis Noël.

One then passes, to the north, a mosaic-fronted butcher's shop to reach the large main square, the place du Maréchal Foch, dominated by a massive 1841 Hôtel de Ville in a late classical style by Lefranc, containing cool classical statues by Louis Noël and Lormier. Nearby stands the old bailliage (bailiwick, or bailiffs' court) which is not what it sounds, but a tall, elegant town-house built in 1786, its balustrade adorned with statues of the cardinal virtues. Leading off the square is the rue des Clouteries with an old-fashioned cake shop, the Patisserie Cramet. The main shopping street, the rue de Dunkerque, has a shop front with grotesque carved heads. Nearby, in the rue St Sépulchre, is the Hôpital, with a pilastered facade of 1702, while in the rue Edouard Devaux the recently renovated Brewery has its gleaming copper vats on view from the street. The best way to leave St Omer is along the Dunkerque road, the N28, with its terraces of pretty cottages overlooking the canal, now sadly empty of boats.

St Omer: Excursion

East of St Omer are the **Watergangs**, created early this century. These intensively cultivated marshlands are intersected by a complex network of little canals for drainage and access. Famous for flowers and vegetables, particularly cauliflowers, they can be visited by boat. The watergangs were a haven for weary First World War soldiers, who went fishing, boating and drinking in the numerous *estaminets* while on leave from the Front. An earlier refugee was Thomas à Becket, who sought asylum from Henry II in the abbey of St Omer. At **Clairmarais**, on the edge of the forest of Rihoult – a preserve of deer and wild boar – the abbey farm is a large and picturesque ensemble with a turreted farmhouse, some huge ancient barns and a dovecote all set around an enormous working farmyard, entered through old gateways.

Take the N42 to the small industrial town of **Arques**, long noted for the manufacture of crystal glass. The bustling quayside, busy with barges unloading sand at the glass works, is a must for lovers of canals. On the other side of the water is the imposing Ascenseur des Fontinettes, a boat lift, constructed in 1888 to lift barges vertically to forty feet, thus bypassing a flight of locks. With its two great tanks or chambers designed to counterbalance each other, it was built by Edwin Clark, and based on his 1875 boat lift at Anderton in Cheshire; it remained in use until 1967, when it was replaced by one huge lock. It is now preserved as an important industrial monument, with a barge in one chamber, and a small museum below.

Taking the N42 onwards to **Renescure**, one passes an attractive Flemish turreted château; at **Ebblinghem**, just off the main road, the quiet village square is dominated by a grand eighteenth-century manor house (c1770) which would look quite at home in Wiltshire.

To the north of St Omer, canal enthusiasts should make a point of visiting **Watten**, which is best approached by the road that runs alongside the waterway. The huge barges known as *péniches*, many loaded to the gunwales with coal or grain, chug

CLAIRMARAIS: The abbey farm

their way continuously past this little industrial town, which has grown up around an important waterway junction. Other boats line the old quays. Watten itself has plenty of atmosphere, blending Flemish tradition and evocative period details such as the lettering of the Café au Centre.

To the south, the D226 leads to a high wooded hill, crowned by a tower – the most visible remains of a former abbey. On the way is a 1731 octagonal stone windmill. The view is excellent – a panorama of forest, flat farmland and intersecting waterways.

Military historians should then travel on to **Eperlecques**, to the west, where, in the woods, is a huge concrete bunker, the Blockhaus d'Eperlecques, claimed to be the largest in the world. Built in 1942–3 by slave labour for the launching of von Braun's V2 rockets to destroy London, this grim brooding fortress incorporates over a quarter of a million tons of concrete, and has a sixteen-foot-thick-roof. Now a memorial to the thousands who suffered during its building, it can be visited. An audio-visual show describes its short and luckily unsuccessful history – had it achieved

WISQUES: The monastery of St Paul

its purpose, little of the centre of London would have survived – and shows it to have been a precursor of Cape Canaveral. Perhaps one day this gloomy structure will become as mysterious as the Pyramids, but for the time being its evil intent is all too evident, and depressing. (For future reference: the blockhouse at **Helfaut-Wizernes**, 7 kms south west of St Omer, is being turned into a war museum, due to be opened in 1992.)

Take the D208 west from St Omer, enjoying, as the road climbs up to **Longuenesse**, the splendid views of the town and the countryside beyond, and continue on to **Wisques**. Here, in a pretty village spread over the hillside, are two abbeys. The first, Notre Dame, is a Benedictine convent, and a rather gloomy nineteenth-century pile; much more interesting is the Benedictine monastery of St Paul nearby. This is housed partly in an eighteenth-century château with a fifteenth-century tower, and partly in more modern buildings. The best of these, notably the brick cloister, were designed in 1931 by Dom Bellot, a monk who had studied architecture at the Ecole des Beaux Arts in Paris. Although he is surprisingly little known, this pioneer of twentieth century Expressionism produced in 1911, at Quarr Abbey in the Isle of Wight, a work of the utmost originality. (See also the entry for Comines.) This later work is in a similar, highly personal style. Unfortunately, the cloister can only be visited by those coming specifically on retreat, but the chapel and bell tower are worth a look, although they are of lesser architectural interest. The bell itself dates from 1470 and is enormously heavy.

ST QUENTIN (Aisne)

St Quentin is the southernmost of the big towns of the North. The town is geographically nearer to Paris than to Calais, and, though in Picardy, it was under Flemish domination until the sixteenth century. In 1560 it formed part of the dowry of Mary, Queen of Scots.

The best approach is from the south; the huge dramatic bulk of the cathedral crowns the skyline, with the town spreading over the slopes below down to the banks of the Somme. The river is near its source here and merges with the Canal de St Quentin, which is still a busy waterway.

At the foot of the hill, before crossing the bridge over the railway, pause to admire the 1920s Casino theatre, its bold Art Deco facade adorned by two enormous grotesque masks of comedy and tragedy. Below the bridge, in a park, is the huge war memorial – a grey stone colonnaded arch in a severe stripped classicism. The excellent low-relief sculptural frieze depicting the effects of war is well worth careful study.

The river is crossed by a 1920s bridge, a good composition with slim pylons and, at each corner, panels of allegorical nudes, three female, one male, emblematic of four of the great rivers of France. On the other side of the river, the main street climbs up to the town centre – the place de l'Hôtel de Ville. This is a lively square, nicely enclosed by buildings which include a neo-Classical theatre; but most date from the 1920s, as a result of the fire-raising depredations of the retreating Germans in 1918. Some of the buildings have sculptured panels of the 1920s. The main feature of the square is the splendid arcaded early sixteenth-century Flamboyant Gothic Hôtel de Ville. In the centre is an arresting 1897 monument commemorating the famous seige by the Spaniards in 1557. This excellent townscape is floodlit at night, as is the cathedral of St Quentin a short distance away: a thirteenth-century Gothic church, possibly built to the plans of the celebrated Villard de Honnecourt, it has suffered much over the centuries; one can still see the holes drilled by the Germans in 1918 in preparation for blowing it up. The interior has a carved late seventeenth-century organ case, some early stained glass and an octagonal maze in the paving for penitents to traverse on their knees. The main attraction, however, is the sheer immensity of the space, over 400 feet long and 110 feet high.

An essential visit in St Quentin is to the Musée Antoine Lecuyer. This elegant stone building, in the style of Le Petit Trianon at Versailles, houses the famous collection of pastel portraits – sharp characterisations of the society of the day – by Maurice-Quentin de la Tour (1704–88), a native of the town.

St Quentin has much provincial atmosphere – witness, for example, the pretty public garden known as the Champs Elysées with its bandstand. It was perhaps familiar to Matisse who worked as a lawyer's clerk in the town. Whilst convalescing from appendicitis he took up painting and later entered the local art school. Happily, he gave up the law. Nearby a café of the same name has a good 1930s interior. For the butterfly fancier, the Musée d'Entomologie has over half a million specimens.

For a different view of St Quentin and its countryside, take the tourist railway to **Origny**: much of its route is along the valley of the Sambre.

St Quentin: Excursion

The obvious outing from St Quentin is to **Guise** (pronounced Goueeze), 27 kms to the east, passing the fortified church at **Macquigny** on the way. Set on the Oise, Guise is a French version of Saltaire or Port Sunlight, i.e. a town devoted to the service of a particular industry, and created largely by the industrialist concerned. In the case of Guise, the industry was the manufacture of domestic cast ironwork, and the industrialist was Jean-Baptiste André Godin. The small ironworks he established in 1840 grew into one of the world's largest manufacturers of kitchen, domestic and architectural equipment – particularly stoves – with 1,500 people employed by 1880. A man of firm political and social beliefs – a true socialist in the vein of William Morris – Godin was the classic enlightened industrialist, and the

ST QUENTIN: Panel on the town's main bridge

ST QUENTIN: The war memorial – a detail

ST QUENTIN: Memorial of the Spanish siege of 1557

ST QUENTIN: *The St Quentin canal*

Godin factory and its estate is a memorial to his benevolent despotism – or paternalism, depending on your point of view. Apart from the factory, he built apartment blocks and housing for the workers, schools, social centres, a church, a theatre and a shopping centre; all in rather heavy late nineteenth-century brick. Not much has changed visually since his death in 1888: Guise is still Godinville and one can walk round much of the estate – admiring the workers' apartments ranged behind the statue of the founder; visiting the rather inadequate museum, seeking out the powerful war memorial, and climbing up through the gardens above the river to find the florid memorial to Godin and his wife, with loyal workers nobly in support. Sadly, the whole place is now rather rundown, with the new owners, Le Creusot, clearly not sharing the founder's enthusiasm.

The town takes its name from a warrior family who relieved Calais from the English, among other achievements. The château,

completed by François de Guise in the sixteenth century, is a ruined echo of grander days. Old streets add atmosphere, particularly around the church a dull building saved from total mediocrity by a complete and vivid set of 1932 stained glass windows by Raphael Lardeur of Paris. In the centre of the town is a pleasant square, lined with old houses, with a dynamic statue by Amédée Doublemard of the Revolutionary hero Camille Desmoulins, who was born here. Just south of the town, at the intersection of the N29 and the D946, is a striking French war memorial: a large panel well carved with dramatic military figures by Martel.

ST VALERY-SUR-SOMME: Low tide on the estuary

ST VALERY-SUR-SOMME
(Somme)

The bay of the Somme is a remarkable expanse of marshland and mudflats, blending the melancholy atmosphere of East Anglia with the delights of the seaside. The whole area is a bird-watcher's paradise – three-quarters of all known European species have been seen here. The park of Marquenterre (on the north side of the bay close to Rue) has been established for ornithologists.

The best approach is from the south, with the wide vista of the bay, and the distant view of Le Crotoy as one enters St Valery (pronounced Val'ry). It is a pretty town, with brightly painted houses facing the fishing boats and yachts tied up to the quays, and narrow streets of single-storey fishermen's cottages. Its size reflects the great expansion of trade that took place in the nineteenth century, following the canalisation of the Somme to Abbeville. Its

tradition as an important port though dates back to the times of the Romans when salt was traded here.

Up above is the old town, the *Ville Haute*, which still has its medieval fortifications and is entered through two massive gateways, with a series of tight-knit streets of medieval and eighteenth-century houses. A bumpy track leads across the fields to the Chapelle des Marins, were there are splendid views across the bay, enjoyed by Degas during his summer visits in the 1890s, painting landscapes and taking photographs. The chapel's outer walls are covered with carved graffiti, some dating back to the 1880s.

Below the walls of the *Ville Haute*, along a tree-lined promenade, are a number of prosperous *fin de siècle* houses on the water's edge – near the spot from which William the Conqueror set off to conquer England in 1066 with his four hundred ships. The war memorial, showing two rather effete comrades-in-arms clasping each other, is a curious reminder of those days of the First World War when the English forces made extensive use of St Valery as a serving port for the Front Line.

St Valery: South Excursion

Following the bay westwards from St Valery, one passes the little fishing port of **Le Hourdel**, with its lighthouse and views, before reaching **Cayeux-sur-Mer**, a rather dreary resort reminiscent of Peacehaven: there is even a suburb called **Brighton** set among the sand dunes (where one villa is suitably called 'Le Sahara'). The long sandy beach is the main attraction. The villas are decorated with predictable name plaques, such as 'Mes Vacances'; 'A l'Automne', suggesting the melancholy of retirement, rather aptly sums up the atmosphere. The post office is a minor 1920s period piece. Out of the town, to the south, is a picturesque Victorian-medieval model farm complex. Beyond this are artificial lakes created in the seventeenth-century by Colbert, who enclosed inlets with embankments of pebbles on advice received from the Dutch; they are now given over to duck-shooting.

Those more concerned with the preservation of bird life should visit the Maison de l'Oiseau, a museum and bird sanctuary and leisure centre. Cayeux is at the end of the line for the narrow gauge steam train from St Valery – an enjoyable way in which to arrive.

St Valery: North Excursion

Just east of St Valery is the village of **Noyelles-sur-Mer**, another place to have been left behind by the sea. One can arrive there by taking the little steam train from St Valery, to visit one of the most unusual of the cemeteries maintained by the War Graves Commission – the Cimitière Chinois, or Chinese Cemetery. A gateway designed by J.R. Truelove, which looks authentically

ST VALERY-SUR-SOMME: *The Ville Haute*

Chinese, stands at the end of a grassy track, guarding the entrance to the graves of nearly 1,000 members of the Labour Corps who were drawn from north China to work as dockers at St Valery-sur-Somme. Many died in 1919, victims of a yellow fever epidemic, and their gravestones, set in an orchard, carry both Chinese inscriptions and grandiose phrases such as 'A Noble Duty Bravely Done', and 'A Good Reputation Endures Forever'. A few kilometres to the north, at **Ponthoile**, is a roadside monument to the Caudron brothers, the aviation pioneers.

The road round the bay to the north leads to **Le Crotoy**, a very popular resort and fishing port, which claims to have the only south-facing beach on the north coast. Jules Verne wrote *Twenty Thousand Leagues under the Sea* here, and later Colette came here to write a novel. It was visited by Toulouse-Lautrec, and painted by Seurat in 1889. This is an excellent place for sea food, particularly at Chez Mado, the famous restaurant long presided over by the redoubtable *grande dame*, Mado. The part of the town by the

ST VALERY-SUR-SOMME: The train to Le Crotoy

harbour, looking out over the immense bay of the Somme, has its own flavour, but there are few individual buildings of note. Perhaps the almost Art Nouveau La Potinière is worth a glance. On the way out one passes a small park with a bandstand and a sculpture entitled 'The Fall of Icarus' – yet another monument to the Caudron brothers. Leaving behind the post-modernist sewage works you then cross the wide surrounding *mollières*, salt pastures on which are raised the famous *pré-salé* sheep which provide literally pre-salted meat.

8 kms north of Le Crotoy is the one-time sea port of **Rue**, now anchored firmly 8 kms inland. This tranquil small town has a great deal of charm. The principal feature of the central Place is the chapel of St Esprit – a marvellously exuberant Flamboyant Gothic structure built to house a crucifix, which, according to legend, was washed up on the shore in 1101, having been thrown into the sea by the Crusaders in the Holy Land, to prevent its desecration by the infidels. Only a fragment survived being burned at the Revolution. The story is depicted in the

NOYELLES-SUR-MER: The Chinese cemetery

ARRY: The château

chapel by some effective nineteenth-century murals by Siffait de Moncourt, a local aristocrat who lived at the château de Moncourt, on the outskirts of the town. More exciting is the vaulting, the extravagant detail of the facade, and a curious room to the right of the entrance, that now houses the life-size statues that used to adorn the facade before its restoration. Standing around in various sixteenth-century attitudes, they appear to be waiting for some long delayed Gothic express train.

Near the chapel are some picturesque but heavily-restored timber-framed houses, the plain but powerful neo-Classical church of St Wulphy and a striking 1914–18 war memorial by a local sculptor, Emmanuel Fontaine. The massive medieval turreted belfry is a splendid feature closing the view to the south. It houses a small museum dedicated to the Caudron brothers, early aviation pioneers who built locally their first factory in 1912. The collection includes some of their trophies of the 1920s, which are handsomely sculpted, and a charming stained-glass window from their factory depicting bi-planes in flight. At the nearby hospice, the sixteenth-century Gothic chapel merits a visit (ask at the mairie for the key). Below a fine roof of chestnut, like an upturned boat, are beams carved with scenes of wild boar hunting. The chapel is well furnished with limewood pews from an abbey, good statues of saints and, notably, a painting of St Augustine attributed to Philippe de Champaigne.

At **Arry**, 4 kms to the east, along the D938, is the château built in 1760 to the designs of Giraud Sannier, the rather severe facade of which, in rose brick and white stone, can be seen easily from the road. Further east on the D938, having crossed the N1, the château at **Regnière-Ecluse** is in complete contrast. It was rebuilt in the nineteenth century in the Gothic-Troubadour style to the designs of the Duthoit brothers. Just to the south in the village of **Bernay-en-Ponthieu**, on the N1, the picturesque half-timbered former *relais de postes* or coaching inn received travellers such as Victor Hugo, who described its activities in a letter of 1837, Tobias Smollet and Laurence Sterne.

LE TOUQUET-PARIS-PLAGE
(Pas de Calais)

A garden city created by a Yorkshire businessman, John Whitley, for the English. Whitley purchased a tract of land fronting the beach which he named Mayville after Princess, later Queen, Mary and launched Mayville Ltd which proposed a luxury resort planned on very grand lines. Garnier, the architect of the Paris Opéra was a consultant and Louis Pasteur and Sarah Bernhardt were patrons. After a number of setbacks, including Anglo-French tension during the Boer War, and local opposition to the English "seeking to leave their sad island and conquer a corner of France", the initial project foundered. Whitley purchased the château of Hardelot and persevered with his dream. By 1904, the year of the *Entente Cordiale*, an 18 hole golf course was inaugurated and a race-course, athletics stadium and tennis courts were completed. J.D. Fergusson, the Scottish Colourist artist, painted in 1905 a scene of fashionable high jinks.

Le Touquet is something of a Weybridge-by-Sea (or, as the wife of the artist Edward Wadsworth called it dismissively in 1923, a 'French Bournemouth'). Extensive pine woods, which have spread from a few trees planted on the dunes in the 1850s, conceal discreet 1920s and 1930s villas, redolent of inter-war weekending. Polo and tennis parties, drinks on the lawn, a few rounds of golf, a visit to the races or to the casino (at a time when there were none in England), charity balls, and a bit of risqué company are the story of Le Touquet. According to *The Times'* obituary of Janet Kidd, who died in 1989, daughter of Lord Beaverbrook, her first husband decided to teach her the facts of life on their honeymoon in Le Touquet in 1927, by taking her on a voyeuristic visit to a local brothel!

In 1882 the first two villas were built in the wilderness owned by Jean-Baptiste Daloz; by 1912 it had become Le Touquet, and a place in its own right. De Villemessant, founder of *Le Figaro*, is credited with adding Paris-Plage to the name to give it cachet. The Prince of Wales, later Edward VIII, led the dance and others followed, notably the Curzons, the Dudleys and the Queensberrys; the affluent came in their wake. The owner of Selfridges store hired a train to bring his guests. By the 1920s this English colony was all the rage, the devaluation of the franc in 1925 giving them more money to spend. Barclays and Lloyds banks took the opportunity to open branches. A notable social centre was Syrie Maugham's 'Villa Eliza'. Its entirely beige interior, created by the famous novelist's wife, was featured in House & Garden in 1927. Noel Coward, Beverley Nicholls, Gertie Miller and P.G. Wodehouse were devotees. Less glamorous was the time when the raffish Gerald Haxton, Somerset Maughan's lover, ended up naked on the bathroom floor covered with 1000 franc notes won at the casino. In 1940 the era came to an end. Not having bothered to join the evacuation, Wodehouse was taken by the Germans from his villa, named Low Wood, to be interned as an alien.

Trains arrived, including the Blue Arrow, linking Le Touquet to Paris and the coastal ports, and by 1929 it had its own airport. Soon there were two thousand villas and grand hotels to match, attracting such exotic visitors as the Sultan of Morocco, with the Westminster setting the style. Taxis were ruled out, only chauffeur-driven cars were permitted.

King Farouk was a regular visitor in the 1950s, and his departure coincided with the end of Le Touquet as a playground of high society. Today, it promotes itself as an all-year-round resort, drawing an affluent crowd attracted by the luxury hotels and two casinos, the tennis, riding and horse-racing. Some culture is provided by a new museum: the Musée Edouard Champion in the avenue du Golf, which has a pleasing collection of the so-called School of Etaples

LE TOUQUET: The covered market

– the artists attracted to the locality from the 1880s onwards, including English, American and Australian painters, but notably the post-Impressionist Le Sidaner.

Despite the daunting suburbia that now surrounds it, the centre of Le Touquet is full of curious delights, and it is worth penetrating the defensive screen of white-walled villas. In the streets behind the seafront are villas with Art Nouveau details, tile panels and elaborate woodwork in the particular Anglo-Norman style seen at its best at Deauville in Normandy. There are apartment blocks with names like 'Bain de Soleil' and 'L'Albatross', and even one called 'Les Aeroplanes', with the names of pioneer aviators incised into the facade, as well as tea shops and a 1930s cinema; but Le Touquet's best feature is probably the huge curved covered market, a model of a vernacular Art Deco style that blends Normandy with Lutyens. Ideally it should be visited on a Saturday morning, which is market day.

Nearby are two other rather astonishing buildings: the anachronistic Hôtel de Ville by Drobecq and Debrouwer, completed in 1931 in a style abandoned elsewhere years before, and which has something of the atmosphere of a 1930s building in provincial America, an impression heightened by the murals within, which are in a style that Osbert Lancaster might have termed Hollywood-Medieval. Across the road, the Art Nouveauish church of Ste Jeanne d'Arc was completed in 1911. Inside there is good stained glass from both pre-and post-war periods, and a grand altar decorated with figures in relief. The post office is in a similar style. Modern Le Touquet is, by comparison, rather dull, but this dullness may one day seem quite appealing when an English developer has completed his scheme to create a massive holiday village on 1500 acres of Le Touquet. Alas, mass tourism, as so often happens, will probably obliterate any vestiges of the town's former style.

Le Touquet: South Excursion

The coast south from Le Touquet, the so-called Opal Coast, is a mass of rather crude development, so lacking in style as to spoil completely the beach. The main town is **Berck-Plage** (or Berck-sur-Mer), a popular but visually undistinguished resort. Apart from miles of golden sand – which stretch all the way to Le Touquet – there is precious little to catch the imagination. It has certainly lost the character of the fishing village which attracted Boudin to paint here. The many hotels devoted to hydrotherapy give the town a rather clinical air. Not surprisingly perhaps since its most famous citizen was a worthy lady called Marianne Brillard, who started an orphanage in the 1850s to care for sick children who would otherwise have been abandoned; she is commemorated by a vaguely Rodinesque statue on the front, overshadowed by featureless blocks of flats. Her success attracted the Assistance Publique and Berck thus became an important medical centre. Other things to see include the lighthouse and the decorative former railway station of 1909, which was converted to a bus station in the 1930s and stands isolated in a sea of tarmac. Some cultural diversion is to be had at the museum, the Musée Municipal (Wed-Mon 3–6 pm), which contains archaeological finds, local pottery, a charming recreation of a fisherman's cottage interior and a collection of paintings by artists of some renown who were active locally: Charles Roussel, Francis Tattegrain and Eugène Trigoulet. The hard life of the fishermen provided strong images for these artists. The Hôtel de Ville (in the town centre – Berck-Ville, away from the beach) contains enormous murals of 1907–9 by Jan Lavezzari, the sea again providing dramatic scenes.

Le Touquet: East Excursion

Etaples was a prosperous town of some substance in the Middle Ages, but there is not a great deal to detain the visitor today. Spread along the northern shore of the Canche estuary, it is primarily a fishing port, with a good fish market and boatyards where large modern trawlers are still being built. And where, in common with several other Northern ports, old fishing boats are being restored for a huge rally of old craft to take place at Brest in 1992.

Away from the quays there is a central square, and plenty of streets of fairly standard terraced houses. These are worth penetrating to discover the post-war church of St Michel by Pierre Requier, which has good contemporary stained glass by Lardeur depicting the creation of the world. The curiously anachronistic sculpture of St Michael on the facade by Fachard looks pre-war, but is in fact the work of the 1980s. Pause on the bridge over the Canche and enjoy the views of the estuary in passing – and wonder what brought visitors such as Victor Hugo and painters such as Boudin and Matthew Smith to so dull a town. In the 1890s an influx of over one hundred artists came to live in or near Etaples, from England, America, Australia, Russia, Germany and Italy. The most notable of this 'School of Etaples' was Henri le Sidaner. This fruitful artistic endeavour came to an end with the Great War; André Derain spent the summer at nearby Camiers where he was inspired to paint his ambitious work 'The Bagpipers'.

The station, Arts and Crafts with pretty 1920s signs, is worth a glance, but the best thing by far in Etaples is the British Military Cemetery, to the north of the town, on the D940.

On a sloping site between the coast road and the Calais-Paris railway, looking out to sea, Lutyens achieved one of his finest war monuments. Two tall matching arched cenotaphs, decorated with garlands and flags forever furled on each corner and beautifully carved in stone, stand at each end of a high raised terrace – well above the graves of the men of many nationalities who

ETAPLES: Lutyens's war memorial and cemetery

are buried here. There are distinct echoes of Thiepval in the piercing of the arches. But it is, above all, the use of the site that makes so powerful an impression. There was, of course, no fighting in this area, which was far from the Front, but Etaples was one of the major depots of the British Expeditionary Force throughout the war, and most of those buried in the cemetery died in the huge hospital complex nearby. But it was here that the training camp was established, the notorious 'Etaps' with its bullying instructors known as 'canaries' from their yellow armbands, and the redcaps, the military police reputedly ex-boxers and footballers. Their harshness and corruption and the infamous Bullring parade ground caused a mutiny in 1917, sparked off by the killing of a corporal. The enraged soldiery sacked the town, chased and killed a number of military police and allegedly beheaded one NCO. Their ring-leader, Private Percy Topless – the 'Monocled Mutineer' escaped

several times but at the end of a lengthy manhunt was shot in the streets of Dundee in 1920. Many of the insurgents were to die at Passchendale but the full story is still classified information – until the year 2017!

VALENCIENNES (Nord)

Valenciennes is a rather dour town with a particularly hefty style of local architecture, which ponderously reflects a long tradition of industrial wealth based on the lace and textile trades. The over-riding impression is of dull streets lined with over-decorated stone and brick villas. The town was severely bombed in World War Two, which makes it hard to imagine that it was once a town of cultural renown – 'the Athens of the North'. In the eighteenth century Valenciennes had its own art school, academy and salon, and a number of important artists, including

Watteau, Harpignies and Carpeaux, were born here. All are represented in the Musée des Beaux Arts, a handsome nineteenth-century building with an excellent collection of paintings and sculpture which provides the one good reason for visiting the town. The Rubens is a curiosity, featuring a lady particularly well endowed with three breasts, and there is a whole gallery devoted to Carpeaux, the most celebrated French sculptor of the nineteenth century before Rodin, best known for the seductive females he sculpted for the Opéra in Paris. In 1871, both Carpeaux and Dalou, his former pupil, sought political refuge in England after the Commune. Their influence was a major factor in the renaissance of English sculpture in the late nineteenth century.

Also by Carpeaux is the lively statue of Watteau – the lower figures are by Hiolle – set in a small park in the place Géry and rather overshadowed by the rather dull church, much restored in the nineteenth century but extensively altered later. The Hôtel de Ville of 1857–68 was re-built after war damage but, happily, is still crowned by the sculpture of Carpeaux, with additions by Lemaire.

A short excursion should be made to the chapel of the Carmelite convent at No 1 rue Barbusse at **St Saulvé**, a suburb just outside the town, 2 kms north-east on the N30. This extraordinary 1966 structure – the creation of Guislain and Szekely, an architect and a sculptor working in tandem – is a wonderful period piece: a mass of geometric shapes that has managed to achieve the look of an enlarged architect's model. Inside, abstract stained plexiglass in soft colours add to the period charm. The whole thing is now looking a bit tatty, but no doubt modernists will enthuse. It is rather hard to find – it has to be approached through a small gate in a high wall, and is virtually invisible from the road.

The Brasserie Duyck, at Jenlain, south of the town, may be visited. It produces a beer so rarefied that it is bottled like champagne.

Valenciennes: South-East excursion

Le Quesnoy is 17 kms south east of Valenciennes along the D934, and its main feature is the set of seventeenth-century fortifications, virtually intact, by Vauban. Pleasantly overgrown and shaded by trees, the high walls provide an enjoyable promenade, enlivened by views of gardens below. One can appreciate the courage of the men of the New Zealand Rifle Brigade who successfully scaled the walls with ladders under heavy German fire in 1918 – an event commemorated by an indifferent panel set into the wall and approached via a gloomy tunnel. It is a quiet place, only really coming to life when a market or a fair fills the sloping main square.

The principal attraction of the area is **La Potelle**, 3 kms to the south-east, a highly picturesque medieval fortified stone château of polygonal plan, guarded by circular towers and surrounded by a moat – a small lake formed from the river Rhonelle.

Valenciennes: North Excursion

The D169 north west from Valenciennes passes through the great forest of Raismes and St Amand, the first national park to be established in France, in 1968. At the very edge of the forest is the spa which gave **St Amand-les-Eaux** its name.

Exploited since Roman times, its waters have regularly attracted attention for their various curative abilities; visits can be made to the bottling plant. Unfortunately the buildings that surround the spa, including the casino, are terribly mediocre – the 1950s at their worst. Carry on across the Scarpe to reach the town of St Amand, where immediate impact is made by the town's spectacular focal point, the massive 1633 tower of the former Benedictine abbey, founded as early as 635. It grew to considerable size, suffered in various predictable ways and was finally demolished at the end of the eighteenth century, leaving just the tower, which dominates the town and the surrounding countryside. It was designed by Abbé Nicolas Du Bois and is an immense structure, 83 metres high, with several storeys of elaborate Flemish Baroque ornament, crowned by a decorated dome and flanked by two side towers. Both its size and its extraordinary programme of carved decoration – with the five orders superimposed: Tuscan, Doric, Ionic, Corinthian and Composite – make this one of the more bizarre buildings in northern France; and beside it, the town, pleasant enough, pales into insignificance. The famous eighteenth-century porcelain of St Amand may be seen in the Musée de la Faience, and the charming Baroque pavilion, also designed by Du Bois, known as the Echevinage, should be visited. It stands in the park behind the abbey tower.

Valenciennes: South West Excursion

12 kms to the south-west is the industrial town of **Denain**, where the first wide gauge railway in France was laid in 1835. Until very recently this was a major centre of heavy industry, coal and steel predominating, with a close-knit working class community with its own patois called *rouchi* – the very stuff of the novels of Zola. The traditional industries have largely disappeared, only in the last few years, and many of the inhabitants have, perforce, moved away. In the Hôtel de Ville, the Musée Départemental de la Résistance is the tragic record of the appalling events of the last war, and not for the squeamish; on the staircase is a huge and powerful painting by Signac called 'The Demolishers', which the locals regard as an ironic comment on their fate, in the wake of the destruction of their workplaces. A poignant Resistance monument was erected in 1980, to the south of the old church, near the rather forlorn château. The inscription reads 'Ami, si tu tombes, un ami sort de l'ombre à ta place'.

In the town centre is a monument of quite a different sort. The bronze statue of Maréchal de Villars commemorates the hero of a famous victory of 1712 at the Battle of

ST AMAND-LES-EAUX: *The abbey tower*

Denain. The flamboyant Baroque image is actually the work of Gauquié (1919), in complete contrast to his work at Chipilly (q.v.). Tourist circuits have been arranged by the local tourist office, including visits to the rail museum and the mining museum and a tour of the sites associated with Zola.

SPECIAL INTEREST LISTS
A personal selection of some of the best things to see in the North of France.

ABBEYS
Dommartin, St Omer, St Riquier, Valloires, Vaucelles, Wisques

HOTELS DE VILLE – PRE 1860
Aire-sur-la-Lys, Amiens, Hazebrouck, Hesdin, Hondschoote

HOTELS DE VILLE – POST 1860
Arras, Bailleul, Calais, Cambrai, Comines, Lille, Long, Montdidier, Le Portel, Roubaix

ART DECO/MODERNE
Amiens (Ecole des Beaux Arts), Béthune (Hôtel de Ville), Le Portel (Hôtel de Ville), Lille (L'Huitrière and Villa Cavroix), Moreuil (Church), Roye (Church), Le Touquet (Market Hall), Wisques (1931 Cloister)

ART NOUVEAU
Amiens (Hôtel Bouctôt), Cambrai (two shops), Douai (rue Bellegambe), Lille (Maison Coilliot), Le Touquet, Malo-les-Bains, Mers-les-Bains, Roubaix

BELFRIES
Abbeville, Amiens, Bailleul, Bergues, Béthune, Boulogne, Douai, Doullens, Dunkerque, Lille, Lucheux, Péronne, Rue, St Riquier

MEDIEVAL CHATEAUX
Esnes, Esquelbec, Olhain, Nampont, La Potelle, Rambures

CLASSICAL CHATEAUX
Bagatelle, Barly, Bertangles, Cercamp, Colembert, Long, Tilloloy, Le Vert-Bois, Wailly

CITADELS AND FORTIFICATIONS
Amiens, Arras, Bergues, Calais, Gravelines, Lille, Maubeuge, Montreuil, Le Quesnoy

MUSEUMS
Fine Arts
Abbeville, Amiens, Arras, Bergues, Calais, Cambrai, Douai, Dunkerque, Hazebrouck, Lille, St Omer, St Quentin, Tourcoing, Valenciennes
Decorative Arts
Amiens (Hôtel de Berny), Bailleul (Musée Benoit de Puydt), St Omer (Musée Sandelin)
Twentieth-Century Art
Le Cateau-Cambrésis, Dunkerque, Le Vert-Bois (Fondation Prouvost), Villeneuve d'Ascq

EARLY SCULPTURE
Airaines (Font), Aire-sur-la-Lys (Bailliage), Amiens (Baillage), Doullens (Mise au Tombeau), Folleville (Church), Hesdin (Bailliage and Church Porch), Mailly-Maillet (Church), La Neuville (Church), Rue (Church), St Omer (Church), Vermand (Font)

GOTHIC CHURCHES
Abbeville, Airaines, Amiens, Rue, St Omer, St Quentin, St Riquier

CLASSICAL CHURCHES
Arras, Cambrai (St Géry), Le Cateau-Cambrésis, Douai, St Amand-les-Eaux, St Omer

TWENTIETH-CENTURY CHURCHES
Pre-War
Amiens (St Honoré), Bailleul, Comines, Fontaine-Notre-Dame, Lamotte Warfusée, Le Portel, Mons-en-Chaussée, Moreuil, Roye, Sauchy-Lestrée, Le Touquet, Vermand
Post-War
Ailly-sur-Somme, Audinghen, Dunkerque, Estrées, Hem, Le Portel, Maubeuge, Miannay, Oresmaux, St Saulvé

CIVIL MONUMENTS
Abbeville (Statue of de la Barre), Avesnes (1793 Drummer Boy), Boulogne (Statue of San Martin), Calais (The Burghers and Pluviôse), Cambrai (Fénelon), Cap Blanc

Nez (Latham), Cassel (Foch), Douai (Jean de Boulogne) Dunkerque (Jean Bart), Guise (Godin), Landrecies (Dupleix), Lille (Pasteur and Faidherbe), Maubeuge (Battle of Wattignies), Montdidier (Parmentier), Montreuil (Haig), Wimille (Colonne)

CIVIL CEMETERIES
Amiens (La Madeleine), Boulogne (Est), Lille (Est)

WAR CEMETERIES AND MEMORIALS
Armentières, Arras, Bellicourt, Bony, Boulogne, Cambrai, Caudry, Chapeau-Rouge, La Couture, Delville Wood, Dunkerque, Etaples, Flers, Louverval, Moreuil, Neuve-Chapelle, Noyelles-sur-Mer, St Quentin, La Targette, Thiepval, Villers-Bretonneux, Vimy, Vis-en-Artois

INDUSTRIAL ARCHITECTURE
Amiens (Longueau railyard), Arques (Fontinettes Boat Lift), Guise (Godin), Hachette (Steam Pump), Lewarde (Mining Museum), Oignies (Coal Works), Roubaix (Factory), Sangatte (Channel Tunnel)

WINDMILLS
Boeschèpe, Gravelines, Hondschoote, Steenvoorde, Watten

RAILWAY STATIONS
Abbeville, Albert, Bergues, Lens, Roubaix, St Omer

DOTTY ARCHITECTURE
Bailleul Circuit (Aeroplane House), Le Touret

MOSAIC AND CERAMIC TILE WORK
Ambleteuse, Ault-Onival, Desvres, Hesdigneul-lès-Boulogne, Lens (Station), Lille (rue de la Clef/l'Huîtrière/rue Basse), Roye, Wimereux (House Names), Zutkerke

ESTAMINETS
Boeschèpe, Esquelbec, Godeswaervelde

BRIEF BIOGRAPHIES
An Architect, a Sculptor and a Military Engineer Particularly Prominent in the North

LOUIS-MARIE CORDONNIER (1854–1940)

Born 1854 at Haubourdin near Lille and the leading exponent of the neo-Flemish revival in architecture in the North of France. Both his father and his son were architects. Despite architectural trends elsewhere in Western Europe, his historicist style survived until the 1930s, producing buildings which dominate the towns of the North, and which are quite oblivious of the successive Art Nouveau, Art Deco and Moderne styles. His output was prodigious and always conservative in style – initially neo-Byzantine followed by his own particular brand of neo-Flemish-Renaissance. His best known building is The Palace of Peace at The Hague. He was responsible for Hôtels de Ville at Loos (1884), La Madeleine (1885), Dunkerque (1896–1901), Armentières (1925), Comines (1928), Bailleul (1932) and Merville; his churches include St Maclou, Haubourdin (1875); Ste Marie Madeleine, La Madeleine (1888); Fauquissart (1902); Notre-Dame de Pellevoisin, Lille (1906); Notre-Dame des Mineurs, Waziers (1927); St Vaast, Bailleul; St Vaast, Armentières; St Pierre and St Vaast at Laventie; Notre-Dame, Fleurbaix (1929); Notre-Dame de Lorette, Souchez (1932); St Vaast, Feuchy; St Pierre, Merville; St Vaast, Béthune; St Joseph, Lille (1930); and the Basilica of Ste Thérèse, Lisieux (1929) in Normandy. A town planning layout was produced for Hardelot-Plage. He gained a prize for his competition design for the Bourse at Amsterdam and restored the facade of Milan Cathedral; the vast Château du Comte d'Hespel, Bondues (destroyed in 1945) is attributed to him. In Lille he designed the Nouvelle Bourse (1906–1920), the Opéra (1908–1914) and the monument to Pasteur. His public buildings also include the Maison des Mines, Lens and the Halles at

Armentières, both in the neo-Flemish style, but for the Lille Opéra he was obliged to employ a Louis Seize style. For the conservative Flemish he was clearly the right man for the time. His characteristic and immense belfries recaptured the spirit of the age in which the towns had gained their civic liberties.

ALBERT ROZE (1861–1952)

Born in Amiens in 1861. He studied sculpture in Paris and Rome and returned to his native city to head the Ecole des Beaux Arts and, for 26 years, he directed the Musée de Picardie at Amiens. His enormous output as a sculptor seems to be entirely located in Picardy, and above all in Amiens itself. He was responsible for numerous portrait busts in a conventional academic style and numerous funerary monuments in the cemetery of La Madeleine, Amiens, mostly conventional with the notable exception of the extraordinary monument to Jules Verne. He undertook numerous commissions for war memorials at Airaines, Corbie, Amiens, Moreuil, Domart-en-Ponthieu, St Acheul Cemetery and Friville-Escarbotin. His best-known work is the Golden Virgin on the tower of Notre Dame de Brebières, Albert.

SEBASTIEN LE PRESTRE, MARQUIS DE VAUBAN (1633–1707)

Born in the Morvan, in Burgundy, in 1633, of an impoverished gentry family and one of the most familiar military names to all French children. As one of Condé's officers, in revolt against the authoritarianism of Mazarin, he was incarcerated, but later transferred his allegiance to Louis XIV and joined the commission for military fortifications. Rising swiftly through the ranks, he became one of Louis XIV's most valued officers, and was created Marshal of France in 1678. For his successful direction of some fifty sieges, he was rewarded by the king with a large prize, with which he purchased the château of Bazoches, in Burgundy, which is still in the hands of

Marble bust of Vauban

the family. As a military engineer, his output was enormous, repairing over three hundred fortifications, mostly on the borders of France. His supreme achievement was the design and construction of tremendous star-shaped citadels, notably those of Lille and Arras. Soldier, town-planner, military engineer, agronomist and architect, Vauban later turned to economics and politics, and published numerous treatises, with unhappy results. Concerned by the misery of the people, his last work, *La Dîme Royale*, proposed more equitable taxation. The king ordered its destruction and he ended his life in disgrace.

BRIEF GLOSSARY OF TERMS

ANGLO-NORMAN
A blend of an English Edwardian half-timbered style with traditional Normandy features, used for expensive buildings in fashionable resorts such as le Touquet and Deauville, from the turn of the last century.

ARTS AND CRAFTS
An idealistic movement of the second half of the nineteenth century, whose best known figure was William Morris, aiming to lead design away from the mass production of the industrial age, and urging a return to medieval standards of craftsmanship. This led to a domestic and vernacular building revival at the end of the century, which had a wide influence and was much admired on the Continent. There is no equivalent term in French, and it is used in this book to classify conveniently certain buildings which reflect this style.

ART DECO
The style, prevalent in the 1920s and 1930s, takes its name from the 1925 Paris Exposition des Arts Décoratifs although its roots are in the pre-First World War buildings of architects such as Perret, Sauvage and Hoffman: for example the Palais Stoclet in Brussels, 1905. Its main characteristics are a strong vertical emphasis, often with zig-zag and angular motifs, and sometimes with sculptural or ceramic relief panels. Showy and sometimes superficial, it dominated applied and decorative arts and fashion in France, even though some of the best Art Deco buildings are to be found in America, especially in New York. It was popular rather late in England and was favoured for cinemas, factories and hotels, for example the Odeon cinema chain, the Hoover factory, Perivale and the Strand Palace Hotel, London. The best example in the North of France is the church at Roye.

ART NOUVEAU
A free style of art and architecture with flowing and sinuous lines based on plant forms, it was mainly developed on the Continent from the 1890s until the Great War. Leading exponents were Horta in Belgium and Guimard in France, best-known for his Paris Metro entrances but with an outstanding example in the North of France, the Maison Coilliot in Lille. The style was called Jugendstil in Germany, Sezession in Austria, Stile Liberty in Italy and Modernismo in Spain. Although it had its roots in the English Arts and Crafts Movement, it was not much adopted in Britain though notable exceptions were Charles Rennie Mackintosh in Glasgow and the sculpture of Alfred Gilbert, whose best-known work is the so-called Eros fountain in Piccadilly Circus.

BAROQUE
The theatrical and voluptuous style of the seventeenth and eighteenth centuries, emanating originally from Italy and especially from Rome. Calculatedly emotional, its Southern and Catholic origins made it difficult for it to be widely accepted by the Protestant countries of Northern Europe, though it was brilliantly executed in England by Hawksmoor, Vanbrugh and Archer. Its appearance in the North of France at Lille and Arras was due to the Spanish occupation. The Jesuits built several Baroque chapels in the North of France – a good example is at Cambrai. The Roman Baroque is uncommon in the north of France, but a notable exception is the high altar in Amiens Cathedral.

CUBISM
A movement in painting started by Picasso and Braque from 1907, breaking away from traditional representation. It was a precursor of modern abstract art.

EXPRESSIONISM
A short lived movement after the Great War, which in architecture was probably

influenced by the buildings of Gaudi in Spain. It flourished mainly in Holland and Germany; Berlage and Behrens were pioneers of this powerful style, with its strong, often organic lines. Bellot produced virtuoso buildings at Quarr Abbey, on the Isle of Wight, the cloister at Wisques near St Omer, and the church at Comines. The Vimy Memorial is a major example of an Expressionist monument, while the church of Sauchy-Lestrée is a rare example in the north of France of the style used for a modest building.

FLAMBOYANT GOTHIC
The last phase of Gothic in France, dating from the fifteenth century, it is characterized by elaborate flowing flame-like tracery, and is well demonstrated by St Esprit at Rue.

MISE AU TOMBEAU
The French equivalent of the Entombment, the depiction in sculpture of the placing of the body of Christ in the tomb. There is a notable example at Doullens.

NEO-CLASSICAL
Prevalent mainly from 1760. An imaginative reworking of pure antique classicism, developed in England by such architects as Robert Adam and 'Athenian' Stuart. Much used later for public buildings, and to be seen in the north of France in numerous châteaux and hôtels de ville.

RENAISSANCE
From the Italian for rebirth. A revival of arts and letters, based on classical models, which originated in Northern Italy in the early fifteenth century, notably in Florence. This cultural revolution spread eventually throughout Europe. It brought respect for the artist and his genius as an inspired creator, often under the patronage of powerful lay figures. The major artists include Giotto, Brunelleschi, Alberti and Donatello from the early Renaissance and, later, Michelangelo, Raphael, Bramante and Leonardo da Vinci of the High Renaissance, when the focus moved from Tuscany to Rome. The post-Renaissance style of the late sixteenth century was called Mannerism, which gave way in the early seventeenth century to the Baroque. The Renaissance is not widely represented in the North of France, but examples include the Hôtel de Ville and Notre-Dame at Hesdin, the tombs at Folleville and the *mise au tombeau* at Doullens.

REREDOS
The screen behind the altar normally carved in wood or stone and depicting a religious scene. There is a good example in the Chapel of St Esprit, Rue.

ROCOCO
After the death of Louis XIV in 1715, a reaction to the excess and formality of Versailles produced, in art and architecture, this stylistic phase of the late Baroque. Elegant, gay, and lighthearted, using small curves for its effect, this short-lived style was essentially French, principally used for interior decoration, with relatively little currency elsewhere in Europe, except in Southern Germany and Austria. Watteau, Boucher and Fragonard are quintessential Rococo artists. The Hôtel de Beaulaincourt at Béthune and the chapel of the abbey of Valloires have Rococo features. The fashion petered out after the 1760s, to be replaced by the more earnest Neo-Classical style.

BIBLIOGRAPHY

Michelin Map 236: Nord – Flandre–Artois-Picardie

Michelin Green Guide: Nord de la France (text in French only)

IGN Map: Pays du Nord – Carte Touristique

For food and hotels consult the Michelin Red Guide, the Guide Gault et Millau, the Guide des Logis et Auberges de France. They are all published annually. The Logis Guide and all general tourist information is available free from the French Government Tourist Office, 178 Piccadilly, London W.1.

Good town maps and information leaflets are available from the local tourist information offices, to be found in nearly all towns in France and denoted on town maps in the Michelin Red Guides. The best town maps are the Plans-Guides Blay.

Travellers' Guide to Art: Volume for France, Michael Jacobs & Paul Stirton (Mitchell Beazley, 1984)

The North of France, F. Tingey (Spur Books, 1978)

The Blue Guide: France, (A & C Black, 1988)

The French, Theodore Zeldin (Flamingo 1984 – Fontana Paperbacks)

France in the 1980s, John Ardagh (Penguin/Secker & Warburg, 1982)

Promenades, Richard Cobb (Oxford University Press, 1980)

That Sweet Enemy, Christopher Sinclair-Stephenson (Jonathan Cape, 1987)

Writers' France, John Ardagh (Hamish Hamilton 1989)

Living in France Today, Philip Holland (Robert Hale Ltd., 1985)

The Identity of France, Vol 1, Fernand Braudel (Collins, 1988)

Cross Channel, Alan Houghton Brodrick (Hutchinson & Co., 1946)

French History & Society, Roger Mettam & Douglas Johnson (Methuen, 1974)

The Great War and Modern Memory, Paul Fussell (Oxford University Press, 1975)

Before Endeavours Fade Rose Coombs (Battle of Britain Prints Ltd., London 1986)

Silent Cities, Gavin Stamp (R.I.B.A., 1977)

The Somme – Then and Now, John Giles (Battle of Britain Prints, 1986)

A Guide to the Western Front, Victor Neuburg (Penguin, 1986)

Holt's Battlefield Guides, T & V Holt (Sandwich, Kent)

The War Artists, Meirion & Susie Harries (Michael Joseph, 1986 – in association with the Imperial War Museum)

A New Guide to the Battlefields of Northern France Michael Grover (Michael Joseph, 1987)

The Unending Vigil – A History of the Commonwealth War Graves Commission Philip Longworth (Leo Cooper/Secker & Warburg, 1985)

Poetry of the World Wars – edited Michael Foss (Michael O'Mara, 1990)

Courage Remembered (The construction of the Commonwealth's Military Cemeteries and Memorials) Edwin Gibson and G. Kingsley Ward (HMSO 1989)

Memoirs of an Infantry Officer Siegfried Sassoon (Faber 1989)

Undertones of War Edmund Blunden (Penguin 1989)

The War Poets Robert Giddings (Bloomsbury 1988)

An Onlooker in France – 1917–19 Sir William Orpen (Williams & Norgate, 1921)

The Face of Battle – Agincourt, Waterloo, Somme, John Keegan (Penguin)

Goodbye to All That, Robert Graves (Penguin)

The following will most easily be obtained from the specialist French bookshops:–

Ouvert aux Public – Châteaux, Abbayes et Jardins Historiques (Editions de la Caisse Nationales des Monuments Historiques)

La France et Ses Trésors – volume for Flandre/Picardie, Sylvie Girard (Librairie Larousse Paris 1988)

Decouvrez le Nord, Monique Teneur van Daele (Westhoek Editions Dunkerque 1985) Companion volume for Pas de Calais is due to appear.
Aide-Memoire d'Histoire de France, Jean Berthier (Bordas 1989)
Histoire du Nord & Pas de Calais – de 1900 a nos jours, Y.M. Hilaire (Privat 1982)
Guide Touristique de l'Industrie, Victor Belot (Pierre Horay Paris 1981)
Pays et Gens de Picardie, Flandre et Artois (Larousse/Selection du Reader's Digest, Paris 1983)
Les Guides des Châteaux de France – volumes available for Nord and for Pas de Calais, Jacques Thiebaut (Editions Hermé Paris 1986)
Eglises et Abbayes d'Artois et du Boulonnais (And other titles in the same series) Philippe Seydoux (Editions de la Morande 1981)
Beffrois et Carillons – Nord/Pas de Calais, (Assecarm Lille 1988)
Le Siècle de l'Eclectisme – Lille 1830–1930 and companion volume: *Les Châteaux de l'Industrie*, (Editions du Moniteur Paris 1979)
14–18 Monuments ou Les Folies de l'Industrie, J.M. de Busscher (Editions des Archives d'Architecture Moderne Brussels 1981)
Les Batailles de La Somme, Marcel Carnoy & Jean Hallade (Editions Tallandier Paris 1988)
Le Vitrail dans le Pas-de-Calais 1918–1939, Patrick Wintrebert (Archives du Pas-de-Calais 1989)
Mosaïque en Baie de Canche, Bernard Maire (Le Touquet 1989)
Le Guide du Boulonnais et de la Côte Opale, Dominique Arnaud (La Manufacture, Lyon 1988)

There are certain books which are not concerned with the North of France but should be read by anyone with a love of France, such as, *The Generous Earth*, Philip Oyler (Penguin), *Le Grand Meaulnes*, Alain-Fournier (Penguin Modern Classics), *Clochemerle* and *Clochemerle-Babylon*, Gabriel Chevallier (Penguin). More light-hearted is *Major Thompson lives in France* (Penguin).

Two well illustrated books which attractively portray France are: *Rural France* by John Ardagh (Century 1983) and *Terence Conran's France*, (Conran Octopus 1987).

Books by Elizabeth David should be read for an appreciation of French cooking, that important aspect of French life, for example, *French Provincial Cooking*, *French Country Cooking*, and *An Omelette and a Glass of Wine* (Penguin). Also useful are *Eating & Drinking in France Today*, Pamela Vandyke Price (Tom Stacey Ltd. 1972) and *The Food Lovers Guide to France*, Patricia Wells (Methuen 1988).

BOULOGNE: St Nicolas 1819 by Capt. Robert Batty

INDEX OF PLACE NAMES

143